Author Acceleration:
Overcome Author Obstacles and Write Books Your Readers Will Love

By Krista Dunk

100X PUBLISHING

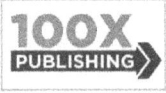

Author Acceleration
© 2020 by Krista Dunk
www.internationalpwa.com

This title is also available in Kindle format.

Published by 100X Publishing
Olympia, WA
www.100Xacademy.com

ISBN: 978-1-7339893-1-2

Printed in the United States of America
Cover background image credit: designed by Idea.s - Freepik.com

"*Author Acceleration* is a book that you need to have at your fingertips. Krista Dunk has created a very thorough handbook, covering every aspect of an author's journey. She has a unique way of explaining each task in a way that inspires the reader with confidence to complete their project well. If you are a new author, or if you have published a few books already, *Author Acceleration* is a must have!"
— *Dr. Cindy Holman, Author, Educator*

"Krista guided me through the writing process from A to Z and assisted me with the parts that I wasn't excited about, like editing. She was extremely efficient which gave me momentum through this experience. Krista not only served as an editor but as a consultant, mentor and advisor. Her knowledge of the industry helped me avoid pitfalls and potentially costly mistakes that could have slowed down the process. She helped me with the book launch and promotion to secure a #1 release and #1 best-seller badge in multiple categories on Amazon."
—*Josh Khachadourian, Author, Founder www.standard59.com*

"Three weeks ago, God told me to turn my journal into a book. I was TERRIFIED, overwhelmed, and honestly not sure where even to begin. In just 10 days, I have written 45 pages, started a Facebook community that already has 40 members...and most importantly, I no longer feel overwhelmed. Krista is a wise and patient teacher who so graciously pours into her students and guides us all the way through the process!"
—*Rachel Jenks, Author, Owner of Brand Boss Studios*

"I've had the good fortune of working with Krista Dunk in a number of ways. As a participant in her 10-Day Write Your Book Challenge, I gathered the inspiration and confidence I needed to move forward with a book I had begun. As a member of Author Acceleration Academy, I've learned a tremendous amount not only from Krista, but also from her guest speakers and other participating authors and aspiring authors. Each session provides me with information I greatly need, valuable insight and new ideas that I would have never considered. Lastly, through her one-on-one services, I've had the benefit of Krista's personalized support to get me over the finish line with my very first book. I will rely on her expertise again as I continue to grow as an author and will be certain to recommend her courses and coaching to others."
—*Patricia Roberts, Author of Route 529*

Dedication

This book is dedicated to all those with a message to share, with a story to tell and with creativity to release. May your words be blessed and your impact be far-reaching.

Table of Contents

About This Book

Although I believe this book will be very helpful for you during your book-writing journey, there's no possible way it can contain everything there is to know about planning, writing, publishing and selling books. If it did, it would have to be an overwhelming 500 pages or more. Even then, with so many types of books and genres, it would still fall short of comprehensive information.

My goal is to get you off to the right start and to overcome common book-writing obstacles many authors experience. I also want to give you ideas, strategy and perspective you may not have considered before so you can write amazing books that impact many.

Being an author has been one of the most enjoyable and interesting things in my life so far. At the time of first publishing this book, I had written nine books. Now, in 2024 I have twelve, with more to come. For me, I truly enjoy sharing my creativity, experience, ideas and knowledge with others, hopefully inspiring them to do the same. Being an author has given me this opportunity.

Along with writing, much of my time since 2012 has been working with authors in a variety of ways, such as hosting author workshops and retreats, teaching classes, offering online book challenges, author coaching, creating book templates to make writing certain types of books faster and easier, working on many publishing-related tasks like editing, book covers, formatting, working with printers, etc., to help authors publish their books, and even certain types of marketing services. As I like to tell people, it's pretty much the best job ever! Having the opportunity to be part of someone's book-writing and publishing journey has been a gift and a joy. Bringing an idea to life is something special.

Are you ready to bring your idea(s) to life? How many books do you have in you? How many messages and stories are you carrying around that need to be told? With a little bit of guidance, know-how and accountability, you can achieve your dream of being an author (or writing your next book if you already are).

Let's get started!

Krista Dunk,
Author, Publisher, International Prophetic Writers Association (IPWA) Founder, www.internationalpwa.com

_____

Chapter One:

Why Write a Book?

Whether it's for the love of writing, because of the love for our readers or both, some of us are meant to be authors and impact others through the written word. For a millennia and beyond, books have signified knowledge, and in early times, those who owned them were typically wealthy. Ancient writings on scrolls were the source of learning and history, along with inspiring people's imaginations and faith.

Now it's your turn to join the ranks of scholars, teachers, philosophers and scribes. I have heard this statistic: Only 1% of people write books. If you're going to be part of this exclusive 1%, the big question is, *why* are you writing a book?

Maybe you're writing a book because...

God told you to.
You have a genius idea that has to get out.
You're a teacher with a new curriculum.
Your personal stories may help someone find freedom and hope.
You've discovered a breakthrough process.
You love creative writing and expression.
You need a book for business purposes or customer leads.
You're a pastor turning a sermon series into a book.
You have knowledge to share.
You're a speaker who needs a book to sell at the back of the room.
You're obsessed with writing a literary masterpiece.
You want to publish a book that becomes a movie.

It's always been a dream or bucket list item of yours.

You want to leave a legacy.

Being an author is cool!

> *Your stories are some of the most valuable things you own.*

The way I see it, writing a book is like sharing an intimate piece of yourself with others. It's revealing pieces of your inner world. It's a form of expression; expressing emotion, creativity and/or beliefs. It's an amazing way to deposit something valuable into others.

Millions of people have written books over the centuries, and authorship has been especially prolific in the last several decades. If those people have done it, why not you? Options for publishing books are expanding, and I suspect the options and formats will continue to grow over the years. There is no shortage of opportunity.

As we get started, I have a few questions for you, the first one being:

How long have you been thinking about writing?

I once had the pleasure of helping a woman named Dolly publish her first book. Dolly was 91 years old at the time. Years of journaling gave her a great wealth of wisdom and stories to work with. I imagine myself being like her when I grow up—still creating, learning and doing amazing things. Another author named Keith told me he'd had his manuscript in his nightstand drawer for 30 years. Over the years, dozens more people have lamented to me about their half-written novel or manuscript, left suspended in time.

Does this sound familiar? In a way, I hope not, but if it does, I'm very glad you are reading this book! You can realize your dream of becoming an author (or getting your next book out if you already are one). It's not too late. No matter how long it's been or how old you are, if Dolly and Keith did it, even after many decades, so can you.

> *"I will write until not a single word remains in my soul...*
> *Until every story in my heart has been told...*
> *Until my mind's well of ideas is bone dry...*
> *And even then I will write on because writing is not*
> *just something I do but part of who I am."*
> —Kathy Jeffords

Whether it's a dream, a bucket list item, a calling or a hobby, writing a book is something many people say they want to do. But again, only 1% will. Are you in the 1%?

Here's my next question for you (with many potential answers):

What are you writing for?

To grow or start a business?
To be known as the expert in your field or industry?
To get more opportunities as a speaker?
To have a resource to sell as a speaker?
To add resources to your ministry?
To share your testimony and inspire hope?
To support or start a cause or movement?
To create a resource for group study?
To influence and impact readers?
To create a popular series?
To inspire creativity in others?

To leave a legacy?

Because it's who you are?

Authors write for so many reasons. So, what's yours? When I started writing my first book, *writing a book* really wasn't on my mind at all. My intention wasn't necessarily to become an author; I just had something to say. So, I sat down, opened up a Word document and let my thoughts flow. Every few days I would open it up and add to it.

At some point along the way, the thought came to me: *I'm writing a book*. The next thought came shortly thereafter: *I don't really know what I'm doing. How do I write a book?* Later, I'll explain more about what I did to gain the knowledge, understanding and help I needed to accomplish the project.

For that first book, *Step Out and Take Your Place: How to Discover and Live Your Everyday Calling*, I wrote to share my experiences and journey, hoping to inspire others to take a journey of their own. There are also two companion resources I decided to create to accompany the main book: a workbook and journal. Because of this being a themed set of three books and the way the content is structured, it has been used by many for individual or group study.

Since those first three books, I have written six more. Some of them are stand-alone books, and some are part of another set created for a group coaching program. With nine books under my belt, is that enough? Do I think I'm done writing? No way! For some reason, I still find myself with *something to say*...

Many of my books have had different audiences/target readers, which makes me wonder:

Who are you writing to?

We're going to broach this topic a lot more in a few minutes, but for now, I'll leave you with some ideas. Here's what I know for sure: You are writing to a person. This person is of a certain age, and possibly of a certain lifestyle, financial category or geographical location. They have certain goals, needs, interests, wants, or problems. They have a certain type of personality and are interested in certain types of things. Are you writing to:

Single moms who struggle with their finances?
Preteen boys who enjoy sci-fi themes?
Twenty-something guys who are avid outdoorsmen?
Women with shame who want emotional healing?
Baby Boomers looking for second career ideas?
People who love WWII historical fiction?
Married couples who need help with communication?
People who want to learn how to become travel writers?
Military veterans who suffered injury?
Preschoolers who like stories about cats?
Entrepreneurs who need new online marketing skills?
Elementary school-aged kids who like science projects?
Christian women who want to learn more about prayer?

I think I could write a 100-page book filled with nothing but lists of different potential target readers. We'll talk more about this later in the book, but for now, keep this in mind when it comes to determining who you're writing to: be *very* specific. Have you thought about who your perfect reader is yet? Who you're writing to determines a lot about the *way* you'll write. You'll want to be sure you write in a way that connects well with that person.

What's stopping you?

This might be a tough question, but if you have the dream or goal to write a book, why haven't you completed it yet? The fact that you're reading this book leads me to believe you're serious about it. I applaud you for reading. However, I don't want you to be a person who just collects information and data but doesn't take action on it.

Over the years of helping people with their writing and publishing goals, several common issues seem to stop authors in their tracks. Here they are:

Time
Money
Know-How
Self-Image
Sensitive Content Concerns
Duplicate Content Concerns
Writing Skill Level
Getting Started
Accountability

Let's take a few minutes to talk about each one and some ideas to overcome these hindrances.

Time

From what I've seen, the biggest hindrance for authors seems to be finding the time to write. With all of our modern conveniences making it possible to squeeze more and more tasks into a day's work, writing is often the unessential thing that gets pushed to the back burner. Many people have full-time jobs, families, household responsibilities, hobbies and any number of other daily activities to attend to. Yet, somehow the things we care about and focus on most still get accomplished.

In life, the things right in front of our face get our attention. Salespeople and marketers know this, and that's why they always urge you to *buy it now*. If you don't, you'll probably move on, never to return.

There's really no pain or negative consequence associated with not getting a book done, like there would eventually be if we don't exercise and eat right. So, how can you keep your book project top of mind and in your face so it gets done? Like exercise, eating right and other things we say we want to do, making writing a daily habit is what will help you succeed. Get it into your daily routine. Pick a time of day that works best for you. Maybe your writing time is early morning, on your lunch hour or later in the evening when the house is quiet. Maybe you're a binge writer, who takes large chunks of time to strike while the idea and flow iron is hot.

I'll address this more in coming chapters, but the solution for much of this time hurdle for authors is about setting a consistent habit.

Money

Money is also a typical concern for authors who want to get a book published. How much is it going to cost to publish a book? I hear this question often. Yes, you can expect that there will be costs associated with publishing your book. Even if you want to pitch your book to traditional publishing houses for publication, you'll most likely need a literary agent and a reviewer. Also, there's the cost of purchasing printed copies of your book once it's complete.

When it comes to self-publishing, there are rare occasions when an author has every single publishing and marketing-related skill themselves and don't need to hire help. This is unusual.

At a minimum, most people at least need help with book cover design and want to hire an editor or reviewer of some sort. Many authors want to buy their own ISBN number (rather than getting a free one through Amazon), and some get a Library of Congress Number (LCCN) for their book as well (not required). And then there's book marketing—an amazing undertaking of its own.

Here's what you can do: budget for your book ahead of time. If you're planning to write or you're writing already, do some research and gather information to make a budget for your book project. If you are serious about this author thing, prepare, plan and save now so you're not caught off guard once your manuscript is complete. As much as I'd like to, it's difficult for me to estimate costs for specific parts of the publishing process here, as they evolve with time and vary widely even now.

For example, book cover help from some sources may start at around $100, probably for a simple, front cover design only, but can cost up to $1,000 for a full cover design with original artwork and a few extra goodies. So many options, so many service providers, so many different visions.

Know-How

If you're an analytical person like me, when you start a new endeavor, you want to know everything; you want to have a clear picture of the big picture. Having enough know-how (or lack thereof) can sometimes stop an aspiring author in their tracks. It's true that writing, publishing and selling a book has many steps, strategies and things to know and understand, but don't allow analysis paralysis stop you from moving forward! You can learn on the way.

It's okay to start writing before you know everything. Get some training and guidance. Ask lots of questions; ask those who've done it before. Find an author coach, class or group. If you feel like not having the know-how you need is holding you back, I'd like to invite you to join us at the International Prophetic Writers Association (IPWA). We are a wonderful community to be a part of for online learning, accountability and gaining confidence as an author.

In a nutshell, here's what the book self-publishing process looks like from a 30,000-foot view:

1. Have a book idea
2. Develop and organize your idea
3. Writing
4. Self-editing and review
5. Professional editing
6. Decide on book format(s) (print, eBook, audio, etc.)
7. Complete other publishing tasks (like cover, formatting, etc.)
8. Research and locate printer and online distribution
9. Devise launch strategy
10. Upload files to online distributor(s)
11. Marketing and on-going marketing
12. Companion products and services development (optional)

THE TWELVE
BOOK
STEPS

What are the steps necessary for writing and **self-publishing** a book?

1
Start with a great Book Idea

2
Develop & Organize your book ideal

3
WRITE!

4
Do your Self-Editing & Review process

5
It's time to get Professional Editing for your manuscript

6
Decide on your Book Format(s)

7
Complete all Publishing Tasks

8
Decide on your Printing Company & Distribution Channels

9
Plan your book Launch Strategy

10
Upload Your Book's Files to the online distributor(s) of your choice

11
It's time for Marketing & Ongoing Marketing

12
Develop Companion Resources & Products if you'd like

Would you like to watch a training video about these 12 steps? I've recorded one for our IPWA members, and you're welcome to watch it as well. Visit our IPWA membership info webpage now, scroll down a bit to find the free training video picture, click it, and simply enter your name and email address to get instant access to the 26-minute training: www.internationalpwa.com.

Some of these steps may not have to be executed in exactly this order, but these are the main decisions and major steps along the way. On the #7 *Complete Publishing Tasks* step, as you can imagine, there are quite a few pieces involved—some big and some small. They include things like getting ISBN numbers, book cover design, interior styling and writing the back cover's marketing blurb.

Hopefully this overview helps you see the big picture.

Self-Image

Another stumbling block for authors is something more profound: self-image. Have you ever said to yourself, "Who would ever want to read a book I'd write? Who cares what I have to say? I'm not qualified to write a book. I am not an expert, so I'd feel like an imposter." If thoughts like these or anything similar have run across your mind, you may be dealing with a self-image that has some hesitation. If deep down you can't see yourself as an author, it will be hard to accomplish your goal. Your own self-perception will be working against you, sabotaging your dreams.

Let me speak to that part of you for a moment. Millions of people have written books, right? Yes, so why not you? You could too. You have something to say and offer to others, whether it's an amazing fictional story, sharing about a journey you've walked through, a story of overcoming, skills to teach to others, or so many other examples.

Would you write your book if it only had massive impact on one person's life? And then what if they went on to impact others through their transformation? No one else can tell the stories you can tell. No one is holding you back from your dream of being an author...unless you are.

Be kind to yourself and give yourself grace. What you have to say and share is valuable. You are valuable. Your (written) voice matters.

"Don't forget – no one else sees the world the way you do, so no one else can tell the stories that you have to tell." —Charles de Lint

Sensitive Content Concerns

Here's another potential hindrance some authors have. "So, Krista, I have to write about something difficult and it will expose and reveal some things about people in my life. What do I do?" This is a legitimate concern I hear quite often. Many people have hard, dark or unjust experiences they've overcome in life. Often, telling these stories implicates family members or other close relationships.

This falls into the category of content fears; fears that telling these kinds of stories will cause legal or relational issues. I have a few suggestions when this is the case.

First, watch your motives. Never write for the purpose of blaming or to expose information and situations to *get someone back.*

Write from a place of wanting your readers to get free from their similar pain, which requires you to be free from that pain first. When people write with unhealed hearts, their hurt and pain advises and counsels others. This is not good. It validates victims to stay victims and just invites more people to the victim party. If you find yourself still in a place of pain, rather than writing a book now, spend some time journaling for a while as you go on an inner-healing journey. Many people write for therapeutic purposes.

Second, there is opportunity for you to write a fictional story based on your life experiences. A lot of novelists use bits of their own experiences and relationships to create their stories. This can be a powerful alternative to writing a non-fiction book on the same kind of theme.

Third, it can be a good idea to change names of people, businesses and even locations in some cases. If you have stories that involve clients, children or anyone else whose names should be kept confidential or protected, change them. If you have concerns about legality or being sued because of the people or situations you want to write about, definitely speak with an attorney who is familiar with libel, copyrights, intellectual property or your particular situation.

The fourth option in situations like this is to have some hard conversations. Tell the people in your life you're writing a book that will contain stories about experiences you had in the past. But the most important thing is to tell them *why* you're writing it. Automatically, they may have concerns about family secrets being exposed, may be worried about their image or maybe it will be the first time they're hearing about what you need to talk about. They need to understand you're writing it to help others overcome their challenges, not to expose or blame.

They may or may not support it, and then it will be up to you to decide what to do next. It's your story, although you'll need to weigh it with how it affects relationships important to you. If someone who harmed you has passed away or is no longer in your life, you probably don't even need to worry about this. In that case, write away...

Duplicate Content Concern

"Didn't someone else already write a book on this topic?" Because there are so many books out there, at times authors can feel like theirs would just get lost. Guaranteed, someone somewhere has already written about what you want to write about. What's my typical response? "Who cares."

If I had 20 people in a room and asked them to write a story about a dog, or to draw a picture of a barn with a horse, or to sing a song about a cowboy, there would be 20 distinct stories, pictures and songs at the end. None of them would be the same because no two people are the same. My dad and I used to watch Bob Ross (the poufy-haired, soft-spoken painter) paint on his TV show. We'd record some of the episodes and play them back in slow motion to try and copy his masterpieces. We were literally copying him, yet our versions never looked exactly like his, nor each other's.

The combination of perspective, experiences, creativity, ideas, and vision you have is unlike anyone else's. No two people will ever write books exactly the same. No two people have the same voice. Besides, maybe it's a good thing someone else already wrote about the topic you want to write about. At least you know there's a market who's interested in it!

That brings me to my last thought on this particular concern authors sometimes have. No matter how many people have already written on the topic or genre you have in mind, there are people who only you are called to influence. Maybe your book is the one that will connect with them most. Maybe your book is the only one they'll ever read on that topic and with that message. Maybe you're the one they trust and want to hear from. Maybe your series will be the one inspiring them to do great things. Maybe your voice is the only one they will hear. So, write on, my friend, and don't worry about how many others already have.

Writing Skill Level

Some people who want to write books feel like their writing skills are lacking. Honestly, maybe they are! But, despite the C minus your high school English teacher gave you on your final essay, you can still write a book.

If you are someone who expresses your ideas and stories better verbally, consider speech recognition software or getting audio recordings transcribed. If you want to write, but your grammar skills aren't the best, get help. Hire an editor. Improve your skills through practice, classes, writing groups and reviewer feedback.

I'm not going to pretend everyone with the dream of being an author has stellar writing skills. You know yourself, so be honest with yourself about where you're at now and what improvements you may need. However, don't allow stress about your general writing skills get you down. Like any new undertaking, you may just need to get some help and develop your skills. You have a great message to tell, so just get help!

Getting Started

Strangely, I've heard some version of this roadblock so many times: "I'm having trouble just getting started," "I can't seem to get started" or "I don't know how to get started." At least this last one just requires some instruction: "I just don't know what to do first" is easier to navigate. The others may be a little more complex to understand why you're stuck.

In my estimation, when people feel stuck at the start, they may either have fears they are dealing with or they just don't have a clear plan. Feeling fearful or disorganized (or both) is dreadful for anyone who wants to start something new.

Some of the fears could be directly connected to disorganization. Specifically, I'm thinking of those with perfectionist tendencies. A couple people in my life, names withheld to protect the innocent, er, uh, anyway...they don't love doing anything they aren't immediately good and successful at. Not sure about you, but I can relate to this in a way. Feeling or knowing you're disorganized can stop someone who loves to analyze everything beforehand.

As a side note, someone who tends towards perfectionism or who has concerns about readers seeing into their soul (especially if it contains personal stories and experiences) may find it difficult to ever call a manuscript *complete*. In this case, putting a book out that seems sub-par in any way, with even one error, is too scary. Revealing more than most people know about you can be too.

Writing a book can feel like setting your mind, heart and or soul on a plate for everyone to sample. You have to be okay with allowing people to taste and see; it could change, impact and inspire them. It requires boldness.

But let's get back to talking about the challenges with getting started. When I was writing a book, but didn't realize I was writing a book yet, I had no outline or anything I was going by. Since that book, I've made it a point to start with an outline, even if it evolves along the way. Whether people realize it or not, if you have an outline done for your book, you have actually begun; you have started your book. Taking the time to create an outline before writing does wonders for helping authors feel organized. We'll talk more about crafting outlines soon.

For non-fiction, another issue stemming from disorganization is not having a crystal-clear picture of who you're writing to, what your focused message is and what your reader outcome is. When you are unclear, you may end up writing random, unfocused stuff. Having a purpose statement for your book will clear that all up in a jiffy. Don't have a purpose statement for your book yet? Not to worry, keep reading and you will soon.

For fiction, feeling disorganized may look a little different. It might be feeling like your story still has big gaps, there's no big picture of the complete story arc or you aren't committed to one genre yet. Having a book purpose statement for a fiction book is also a good idea, along with a storyboard or story arc defined.

In any case, there's always a reason why getting started hasn't gotten started. It could even be one of the other issues on this list—the time factor, self-image, content concerns, accountability, or something else. If you're struggling with getting started, ask yourself some tough questions and figure out why, exactly. Once you've figured it out, then you can make a plan to overcome it and get moving forward.

Accountability

Lastly, after having worked with authors for many years now, if this one thing is missing, a majority of authors will never complete their book projects. That one thing is *accountability*. Because book writing is often something unnecessary in life, it can easily be postponed indefinitely.

"The great thing about being a writer is that you have a long, perhaps frighteningly long time in which to do your work."
—Julia Leigh

Every six months I go to the dentist where the hygienist keeps reminding me to floss regularly. "Oh yeah, okay," I think, and it reminds me to keep the habit of flossing. Otherwise, it's easily skipped over and I'm too busy, I'm too tired or whatever else comes up at that moment.

Writing a book is much the same, except without the consequence or pain of getting a cavity. Often, authors don't have anyone telling them to keep going or checking in on their progress. We need other people to stoke the fire of our dreams. Very few of us are masterful at stoking our own fires all the time. We need a clear, time-based goal and a person to hold us to it (to encourage us toward it).

Becoming an author is an amazing goal. It is something good. Our work as authors can make a meaningful difference in the lives of others. We inspire, teach, fascinate and transform. So, what is your plan for getting accountability? Who is going to stoke your campfire?

Push Past it All

Hindrances, stumbling blocks or roadblocks—whatever you like to call them—those nine things I just highlighted account for nearly all of the good ideas and half-written manuscripts that never materialize. Each of these obstacles can be overcome, however, and my hope and prayer is that you'll push past anything standing in your way of becoming an author. People are waiting on the other side of your book.

Show Me the Money

Let's talk about another question you may have. You have probably wondered, do authors really make money? I remember a funny instance after I wrote my first book. One of the teenagers at my church heard that I had written a book and I was now *an author*. Apparently he was impressed, because one day he walked up to me and said, "Wow, you're an author now. Can I have your autograph? Are you going to be rich?" After chuckling for a moment, then realizing he was serious, I replied, "Sure, and I don't know."

On another occasion, I did a how-to-write-a-book training for a group of inmates at a jail. It was an interesting experience to say the least...but during the presentation, I posed a question. "Why do you want to write?" One man, who I could tell was quite a character, spoke up. He said, "I want to become rich."

It's easy to look to the super-successful authors of our time, people like Jack Canfield, Dean Koontz, Danielle Steel, Stephen King, John Maxwell, or Agatha Christie and imagine the dollar signs rolling in. Lots of people have assumptions about authors making loads of money. But does writing a book equal financial windfall? Let me give you the straight truth: maybe, but not often.

For those whose goal is to become rich by simply writing a book and slapping it up somewhere for sale, chances are very low. It takes a lot of consistent effort, skill improvement, market research, help, and mining of marketing and PR opportunities. If someone writes a book, publishes it and only has a hope and pray strategy (which I'm all for hope and prayer, generally speaking), it's most likely going to remain an unknown book.

Have you ever driven out in the desert? Miles of road, thousands of acres of sand and rock, a tree or tumbleweed here and there, and a few driveways that lead to who knows what. At the end of those long, remote, dirt driveways are houses of some kind. An unmarketed book is like a hidden property in the desert. Roads go by (marketing avenues) and yes, it (the book) is connected to the main roads, but passing drivers (potential readers) are not going to venture down some random, dirt driveway. I know I wouldn't.

However, passing drivers might stop if there was a sign saying "HOMEMADE ICE CREAM, 200 FEET ON RIGHT" and a roadside stand was conveniently there. I would! If something I liked and wanted was conveniently in my path, I'd be very interested.

That's our goal: get our books into the path of our target readers. Authors who are the most successful at selling their books have figured out a few things. They know where their target readers hang out online and offline. They continue to talk about their message. They have a website and social media accounts for themselves as an author. They get interviews. They do some live speaking or training. They have an online community of readers interested in their topic or series.

The most successful authors I know have either built businesses around their book/message, or their book(s) fit into a current business they already run. Here are some examples of how this can work.

My friend, Pedro, is a financial professional. Getting leads for his business was expensive, and his marketing efforts didn't always attract the right potential clients. He got the idea to write a book called *Retired and Free* as a lead magnet item he could give away. The book is full of information he'd present to potential clients during trainings and seminars, plus examples of different clients he's worked with and effective financial solutions that worked for them (real names kept confidential, of course). His business exploded once he used this book for attracting clients. He created ads on Facebook and with postcard mailers to local residents touting the free book for anyone who signs up to attend his free financial seminar. It's not for sale on Amazon; people can only get it by attending. He used a book to expand a business he already had by incorporating it into his marketing plan.

Another author friend, Dave, wrote a book called *I Finally Quit, and So Can You* about his personal experiences with being an alcoholic and overcoming alcoholism. While he was writing, he was simultaneously building an online membership community and website where he could encourage people who want to quit destructive habits and addictions. The book is an important piece of his business' products. He sends it to all new members.

An author who I recently helped with editing and formatting has a book she sells when speaking. My friend Jenna's book is called *Uncluttered*. As a speaker for women's groups and ministries, Jenna sells her books when she goes to speak at events and meetings. Being an author is also a great way for people who want to speak to get more speaking gigs.

After writing one of my books called *Make Your Money Work for You*, my husband, a friend and I held a six-week mentoring group for people who wanted to get new perspectives and strategies for financial stability and building wealth. We created more opportunities to help and influence people using the content and information already contained in the book.

If you want to have maximum impact, the book itself is not the end goal. Selling more books might be a byproduct of a bigger plan you have; a plan or business you already have or one you can create to repurpose your book's content. Do you have a current business that would benefit from having a book? Do you have a book idea that you could expand into a bigger business or platform? Could your writing become a popular series or screenplay?

Frankly though, maybe your goal as an author isn't to *go big*. One aspiring author and friend of mine wants to write a book highlighting the Native American tribe he and his wife are members of. It will contain historical information, genealogies, family stories, details about the evolution of their local tribal lands, customs, and more. I like to call this type of project a legacy book. Never meant to be a New York Times Bestseller, this type of book captures information, photos and stories that will be cherished by a specific group of people or family for years to come.

There was another project I helped publish where the author was a woman with decades of quilting projects and photos. After she was diagnosed with a serious condition, her healthy and ability to quilt declined. She and her husband worked together to gather photos and information of each project, when it was completed, who it was for, etc. A project like this is very personal. They created it to honor her years of creative work.

One author I worked with several years ago wrote a book with a political theme. Really, his goal was to finally publish the book he'd had on his heart for many years. He had something to say, and all he wanted was for it to be in print. He had no hopes or dreams of selling thousands of copies. He was completely satisfied to check off his bucket list item of *finally writing that book.*

Your unique goal(s) as an author is really all that matters. Like each book, every author is different and your plan should reflect that. Carefully consider what your objectives are, and then plan from there.

> *"The tragedy of life doesn't lie in not reaching your goal. The tragedy lies in having no goals to reach."* —Benjamin Mays

Now that we've taken some time to talk about why someone may want to write a book, what typically hinders aspiring authors and some benefits of having a book, let's get into some practical tips for getting started as an author.

Chapter Two:

Get Ready

Becoming an author is a journey. With any journey, being prepared as best you can as you embark helps tremendously. Twists and turns will undoubtedly come, but at least everything you confront won't be a surprise to derail you.

Much of what I'd like to bring up in this chapter has to do with getting your environment and mindset right. If I write in a chaotic environment or am not in a good frame of mind, it can affect what and how I write. Maybe you've noticed this yourself. It's also about setting yourself up for success with some best practices. I also have a thought on the possibility that you already have more of your book written than you realize. Read on to find out about that exciting prospect!

Before You Start

As we continue, I have a quick disclaimer. Realize something about this book: I'm letting you know my best practices and some of your options. There's no possible way this succinct book could contain information about every idea, option or service out there when it comes to being an author. This industry, and companies and services within it, changes rapidly. Along the way, I may give some advice and strategies, but it doesn't mean it's the only way. You have options. What I share isn't necessarily the way it must be done, but it is what's worked well for me and others who I have worked with.

For example, one thing I recommend is compiling everything in one Word document—notes, your outline, thoughts to develop more, and eventually use the document to start writing in. But Krista, what about Google Docs? What about Scrivener? What about...whatever? Yes, there are many options for how you can organize yourself and get your manuscript going. I like Word (and many editors will too, FYI), but there are other options.

Getting Started Tips

> *"Start writing no matter what. The water does not flow until the faucet is turned on."* —Louis L' Amour

As you sit down to write, here are some suggestions to help you be successful.

Reduce distraction as much as possible.

If you're someone with small children living in your home, you may have just laughed out loud at that tip. But seriously, your writing environment and frame of mind is important. Even if kids don't live at your house, distractions abound. Email, calls, texts, videos, TV, cleaning, social media, neighbor noise, and so many more things can quickly draw our attention away. In fact, just after I wrote this paragraph, I got distracted on Instagram for ten minutes...ha!

It's not necessary to have everything perfect in your surroundings in order to write though—sitting poolside with your laptop, sunglasses and iced tea, soaking up the sun and peaceful scene (although that sounds lovely)—just know what *you need* to be successful and focused.

Maybe it would help you to have a water bottle nearby? The phone and TV turned off? The kids set up with an activity of their own? A prayer to start off your writing time? All of your email read through and responded to first? Your office door closed? Wear some headphones? A pretty or peaceful scene to look at? Phone notifications turned off? Background music that inspires creativity? Create the writing environment most effective for you and that reduces distraction as much as possible.

Set some writing goals.

Many authors start out with daily or weekly word count writing goals (plus an overall word count goal for the manuscript). Goals are a good thing, but be a bit flexible with yourself. If there's one thing I know about writing goals it's this: you'll have great writing days where you're on a roll and content and stories pour out of you like a waterfall, and then there are frustrating writing days when the writing flow seems blocked or you don't get as much writing time as you'd hoped (or both).

> *"Setting goals is the first step in turning the invisible into the visible."* —Tony Robbins

Think about this: if you could write 5,000 words each day for the next ten days, you could have a 50,000-word manuscript. That may be a bit ambitious for most, and it may actually be a larger word count goal than you really need. One of my manuscripts has just 21,000 words, and I feel satisfied that the book contains everything it needs at that size. Had I tried to make it bigger and add more, it may have become less focused and full of fluff content. There was no need to add unnecessary extra stuff just to make it bigger. The book you're reading now has about 32,000 words. Another one of my books has 60,000+ words. Each of them felt complete.

What if you wrote 1,000 words every day for the next 30 days? This is ambitious, but certainly doable. You'd have a nice-sized, 30,000-word manuscript. This size could be good for some non-fiction topics or possibly for pre-teen fiction. By the way, fiction novels have a minimum word count of 40,000 (usually more like 50,000-100,000), unless you are writing a smaller novella or short story. Non-fiction books can vary a lot, depending on a lot of factors, but normally fall between 15,000-70,000 words.

I would caution non-fiction writers about big books—over 225 pages/70,000 words. Large, non-fiction books can seem daunting to some readers. Don't pile everything you've ever learned, experienced or know how to do all into one book. Resist this temptation! As we'll talk about more in the next chapter, be sure what you're writing is one targeted message to one targeted reader. If you find yourself with a huge manuscript discussing several different topics, you probably have more than one book in there. Many people have more than one book to write, whether it's to the same audience or a completely different one.

Back to my idea of having a daily goal of writing 1,000 words. As I'm working on this section of this book, I will hit 1,000 words written today. Yesterday, I wrote only about 500, and the day before was also about 500. Several days ago, I had another 1,000 word count day. Tomorrow, I have other appointments and won't be able to write much. Am I feeling disappointed about not hitting 1,000 each day? Nope, not at all. I'm feeling quite content, actually, knowing I have been consistently writing each day.

Goals are great and goals are helpful, but they are there to help you make great progress, not to stress you out or make you feel like a failure. They exist to help you keep moving forward toward what you say you want.

To figure out how quickly you could complete your manuscript, you need two details: your desired word count and your writing deadline. If your deadline goal is the priority, count up how many days you have between now and then and do some math. If having a certain word count is your priority, do the math slightly different.

Hypothetical examples:
My deadline to write my manuscript is 40 days from now. I can write 700 words per day. My book's word count will end up being approximately 28,000 (40 x 700) unless I can write more (if I wanted a larger book).
-OR-
My goal is to hit 40,000 words and I'd like to give myself a maximum of three months to write. 40,000 divided by 13 (weeks) means I will have to write about 3100 words per week (or approx. 450 words per day) to hit my goal.

What's going to work best for you when it comes to setting goals? There's no rule, so set a goal that keeps you motivated.

Gather your resource pile.

Here's an exciting thought: is it possible that you already have some of your book written and you don't realize it? You probably have a resource pile.

Gathering your resource pile means finding all the notes, inspiration, statistics, documents, scriptures, presentation outlines, blog posts, audio files, journals, or anything else that may contain already-created content and ideas useful for your book project. Maybe you even have documents in your computer with ready-to-use content. If not, what about these items below?

- Journals – do you have information in your journals related to your book's message?
- Blog Posts – are you a blogger (or were you in the past) with blog posts ready to repurpose into a book?
- Speaking/Presentation Notes – have you presented, trained or spoken before on your book's topic and prepared speaking notes you could refer to and incorporate?
- Audio Files/Recordings – are there recordings of you speaking/talking about your stories, topic and message you could get transcribed?
- School Assignments – have you done school assignments on your topic before?
- Notes You've Taken – do you have notes you've taken regarding your topic that may come in handy? Maybe notes from conferences, trainings, church services or other events you've attended?
- Idea Notes – do you have sticky notes or notes somewhere else where you've written down ideas and inspiration?
- Are there other reference materials, historical information, scripture or other data you want to include?

What's in your resource pile already? This can also include research you've already done, quotes, statistics, scriptures or other items you've identified and plan to include. Gather your resource pile, all of these existing treasures, to yourself as you get ready to write. They will prove useful and valuable!

Got writer's block?

Inevitably, there are going to be days when you sit down to write and it just isn't happening. The blinking cursor on your open document mocks you. If (when) you get stuck, there are several things you can do to jumpstart your flow again. Here are a few ideas:

First, you could do a timed, writing prompt exercise. Many writers utilize writing exercises when they feel stuck, want to improve their skills or just for inspiration. Writing prompts are deep or imaginative questions intended to spark a person's thoughts, opinions, feelings or creativity. Here are a few writing prompt examples you could use:

What injustice bothers you most in the world?
Create a list of 20 things you're grateful for today.
What do I want to be when I grow up?
If I could do one thing and not fail at it, what would it be?

Even some quotes like this one make good writing prompts:

"Most of the basic material a writer works with is acquired before the age of fifteen." —Willa Cather

There are hundreds more prompts besides these to be found on the Internet. When you do a writing exercise, it's best if you don't edit yourself and don't stop writing. Do your best to let whatever flows out, flow out. These exercises and prompts are meant to get your mind and fingers moving, in hopes you'll get past any mental stall you had before.

When doing a writing exercise or prompt, if you suddenly get inspiration for your manuscript, ditch the exercise. Just because the writing prompt said "write down 20 things you're grateful for today" doesn't mean you must complete the list of 20, especially if at number 11 a brilliant idea came to you. Stay flexible. The goal is for inspiration to come.

"If writer's block is staring you in the face, describe its shape, color and texture." —Unknown

Here's another idea. This is one of the biggest writing block buster tips there is: start writing in a different place. Let me share some exciting news with you. There is nothing in book writing 101 that ever says you have to start on page 1 and write only in order. Let that free up your thinking right now! If you have a clear, detailed outline (which we'll talk about more soon), there's no reason you can't decide to write in chapter three today, chapter eight tomorrow and in the introduction the day after that.

Some author coaches will say write only one full chapter at a time until it's complete, but I personally can't do it. My mind doesn't work that way. If it works for you, then by all means do it. But you may be like me, someone who may feel like I don't have anything else to say today in the section, scene or chapter I wrote in yesterday, and if I forced myself to keep going there it would feel hard.

Another fun idea to get past writer's block is to ask yourself this: what would so-and-so say about this point/scene? You probably have someone fun, wise, odd, snarky, dorky, highly intelligent, or some silly people in your life who could be an inspiration for a different perspective on something.

Remember the WWJD (What Would Jesus Do?) bracelets from the 90's? Maybe you're not as old as I am (wink), but those bracelets served as a reminder. They were an exercise in getting into the mind of someone else when you weren't sure what to do, say or think in a certain situation. You can do this as you write!

What would Grandma Jean say about this point? What would Mike do if it were him in this scene? What advice would my Grandma Thea have given here? How would Gloria have seen it? What would Aaron have said about this? What funny phrase would Karissa have used in this situation? Analyzing a point, scene, character or information from someone else's perspective can be fun and may help diversify your content.

Use writing exercises and prompts, your outline and thinking of the quirky people in your life to get you past any writer's block you may experience! If all else fails, go for a walk outside.

Stay motivated.

As an author, how do you stay motivated to keep writing and get published? I've talked with so many authors who've had a partially-written manuscript for years, decades even, and also many more who have an idea for a book they've never started. Have you ever noticed that ideas are fun? To make the idea become reality requires us to actually *do something*, which is where the first pitfall can happen. Have you ever noticed it's a lot easier to start something than it is to see it all the way to completion? Sadly, been there, done that on both accounts.

But one excellent way to stay motivated is to know there are people waiting. I briefly mentioned this thought before. As my pastor says, there are people waiting on the other side of your obedience. Let's change this a bit for our purposes:

There are people waiting on the other side of your book.

I don't know about you, but for me, this is the biggest motivator there is to keep going, to keep writing. You are reading this now because I persevered. Now it's your turn. Tag, you're it.

What you have to say is important. So what if you're not well-known. Is your story, creativity or knowledge less valuable or less important than someone else's? No! For the love of all things good, please be someone who allows what's in you to flow out and impact others, making a meaningful difference in their lives. You can do this.

Besides remembering your readers, one other tip for motivation is to make a book cover (even just a mockup that you may change later) and post it near your desk or favorite writing space. I feel like having the front cover is motivating in itself. One of my favorite online sites/tools for making a cover mockup is Canva. You can make one for free, and like I said, it most likely won't be the final version you use to publish with. Getting a designer's help is the best idea, although for a motivational mockup, no worries. Just make one yourself!

It's fun!

Last on my list of before-you-get-started tips is this: think of writing a book as fun. Honestly, it's pretty cool to be able to say, "I'm writing a book," right? It's something many people say they'd like to do *some day*, and you're actually doing it (or you will be shortly). How wonderful! If you can have the mindset that this book-writing journey is fun, it will help you stay positive.

Book writing is a creative process, but also a logical process at the same time. Just like you allow a deep exhale, let your expression come out. Remember, everything seems hard until you know how to do it. You'll be a pro soon, and it is my sincere hope that this book helps you gain confidence for your journey.

Now it's time to organize all your ideas!

Chapter Three:

Organize

In my opinion, one of the best things you can do for yourself as an author is to organize your ideas and define a few things before you get started writing. I think I've made my case already for how feeling organized helps immensely, but now I want to show you exactly *how* to organize your ideas.

Just like a person who wants to build a new house plans ahead by having blueprints drawn up, locating skilled workers and starting with a strong foundation, your planning phase ensures you will build a great book.

Purpose Statement

I have a powerful tool to share with you as you get ready to develop your book's concept. It's called the Book Purpose Statement. No one ever told me this while writing my first book. In fact, I've never heard anyone give this formula before. I created it, and I'm happy to share it with you.

I believe writing with a clear purpose in mind will help you write a better book—one your readers will love—and write it faster. In order to create a purpose statement for your book, you need to be able to clearly define the following six things:

What kind of book are you writing?
What is your role? Who are you to the reader?
WHO is your target reader?

Main message/topic?
Reader outcome?
Call-to-action?

Let me show you how these all fit together to create a powerful statement and guidepost for you as you write. Each of the six items above fit into the blanks here:

I am writing a _____ (what type of book) book to _____ (verb: help/teach/uplift/train/counsel/influence/inform, etc.) _____ (WHO) about/with _____ (topic/main theme), knowing they will walk away with _____ (desired reader outcome) after reading, and then _____ (call to action).

Can you see how filling in these blanks will bring massive clarity? Now, let's talk more in depth about each one.

What kind of book are you writing? There are many, and here are a few examples: devotional, children's illustrated book, study guide, fiction novel, pre-teen novel, personal testimony, training manual, sci-fi novella, manifesto, inspirational, how-to, lead-magnet, legacy, small group study, anthology, autobiography, curriculum, etc.

What are you doing in this book? What is your role/who are you to the reader? Examples of what you'd put in this spot are actions (verbs) like help, teach, minister to, train, counsel, influence, inform, inspire, uplift, refresh, implore, mentor, coach, etc.

WHO? Who is your target reader? We'll talk a lot more about this in a minute, but this really needs to be specific. Just saying "women" or "businesspeople" is way too general. "Women who struggle with infertility," "businesswomen in their 20's" or "people who want to start an e-commerce business" is much better. And you may think everyone needs to read your book, but not everyone will. "Everyone" is not your target reader. I'll talk more about this in a moment.

What is the main message or topic of your book? The history of golf in Scotland, parenting children with disabilities, learning HTML coding, desert climate landscaping design ideas, sci-fi romance that takes place on a different planet, WWII historical fiction, overcoming an eating disorder, wedding planning on a budget, how to create an Etsy store, discover your God-given calling, developing effective sales skills, learning to be a good friend, parenting teens, adventure novel, or literally thousands of other potential topics!

After reading, what do you hope the reader walks away with? This is the reader outcome. What do they want? What do they need? Hope, new skill, peace, sense of direction, new vision, healed heart, sense of adventure, ability to forgive, realization of their gifts, recovery, sense of wonder, inspired imagination, etc.

What call-to-action does your book have? This is something we'll discuss more in a later chapter, but for now, this is an action step readers should take once they're done reading. Is it something they should do to connect with you more? Should they sign up for your weekly newsletter, hire you to speak for their team or event, buy other books in your series, join your online group, contact you for a free consultation, do business you're your company, visit your website to sign up for the free report or worksheet you're offering, listen to your podcast, sign up for an online workshop or challenge you host, buy a product you sell, etc.? Or maybe it's something else, like to take action on a cause, support an organization or do something personally important to them to help them move forward on their journey.

So right now, take a few minutes to brainstorm the answers to these six questions, then formulate your book's purpose statement. Write it out in one, long sentence. Here are a few examples of how various purpose statements might look:

I am writing an educational training book to mentor Gen X and Millennials about non-traditional investing ideas, knowing they will walk away with a new perspective and ideas they don't hear from traditional financial advisors after reading, and then join our 6-week online financial coaching group.

I am writing a devotional book to inspire Christians who want to know God better about journaling and hearing His direction, knowing they will walk away with new ideas about who He is and spend more time in prayer after reading, and then sign up for my e-newsletter.

I am writing a children's book just for fun for boys and girls ages 3-8 about a ninja cat who guards her neighborhood at night, knowing they will walk away with laughs and excitement after reading, and then want more books in the series.

In case you're wondering, those book purpose statements are real; they're a few examples of actual books I have written over the years! Most of them were written without the Book Purpose Statement tool beforehand, but I'm happy to share it with you today so you can start off on the right foot.

To gain greater understanding, I'd like to take a few minutes to dive into certain parts of the purpose statement a bit more.

WHO:

Defining exactly who you're writing to matters, a lot. Like a business needs to niche down and target a specific type of customer, a book must target a specific reader. In a way, your book is a mini-business. For some authors, their book directly ties to their business, ministry or work.

You may think *everyone needs to read my book*. Well, maybe they should, but they won't. Besides, you're not really talking to everyone. Fiction or non-fiction, you're not really writing for everyone. The stories you're telling won't connect or resonate with everyone. Not everyone will see your book and be willing to pay money for it. Some people just won't care and that's okay. But who will?

This is the key question to ask yourself when it comes to who your target reader is:

Who will pay money for my book because they recognize it's exactly the book they need/want to read?

When you write, having the mindset that you are writing to *one* specific person can help you a lot. Many of us are comfortable having a conversation with, telling a story to or teaching something to one person. Who is this one person you are sharing your wisdom, knowledge and creativity with?

Contemplate things like these as you determine who you are writing to:

Men, women, both?
Kids?
What ages?

People with certain life experiences?
People with certain goals and dreams?
People with certain questions?
People with certain problems?
People who love certain topics and hobbies?
People with certain belief systems?
Geographic location specific?

Keep in mind that you will most likely also have some "fringe readers." These are people who may not be in the center of your target, but may still be interested in your book. For example, when my son was getting ready to go into the Navy to join an elite, special operations team, he wanted to read books about it. If someone wrote a book about how to qualify and train for this team and what to expect once you're in their rigorous training program, my son would be the target reader. But guess what? I would be a fringe reader. Am I planning on taking up a new career in military warfare at this point in my life? Um, no...although I may be curious to read this since someone I care about is.

Who might your fringe readers be? Do not write the book for them, but realize they're out there.

Message/theme/topic:
Generally, what is your book about? Your book's main theme or message will be connected to the genre your book is eventually listed in once it's published and available for sale. You'll have a general topic or theme, plus your unique spin on it. For example, you may be writing a book about marriage. Your unique perspective or message is for couples to create long-term goals together for their family and finances. Maybe it's an adventure book for pre-teens. Your unique adventure story highlights best friends who save their school. There's always a general category,

plus what you have to say about it.

Reader outcome:
Every author writes a book for a reason. There's a purpose behind the words. Great authors write not only for the love of writing, but also to impact, influence and inspire others. You have a good reason for writing your book. There's something you want your reader to walk away with afterward—a change, an idea, a smile. This is what I mean when I mention your reader outcome.

Reader, when you're done reading my book,
this is how I want you to feel,
this is the transformation I want you to have,
this is the new perspective I want you to see,
this is the new skill I want you to have, or
this is the new clarity and understanding I want you to have.

Voice:
I'd like to go on a slight rabbit trail right here for a moment. Beyond having the Book Purpose Statement established for your book, we need to talk about your author "voice." What is the voice you'll use throughout your book? Although voice isn't directly part of your book's purpose statement, it's related to who you are to your reader.

Here's a basic definition of voice found at literaryterms.net: "In literature, the voice expresses the narrator or author's emotions, attitude, tone and point of view through artful, well thought out use of word choice and diction. A voice may be formal or informal; serious or lighthearted; positive or negative; persuasive or argumentative; comical or depressed; witty or straightforward; objective or subjective—truly, voice can reflect any and all feelings and perspectives."

Your author voice is an important aspect to consider. The combination of these four things will determine the best voice to use as you write:

1. Who your audience/target reader is
2. Your book's topic
3. Who you want to be to your reader (non-fiction) or what the typical voice is for your genre (fiction)
4. Your personality

Have you ever heard the concept of *speaking register*? Wikipedia has this definition to offer:

"In sociolinguistics, a register is a variety of language used for a particular purpose or in a particular communicative situation. For example, when speaking officially or in a public setting, an English speaker may be more likely to follow prescriptive norms for formal usage than in a casual setting...choosing words that are considered more 'formal' (such as father vs. dad, or child vs. kid), and refraining from using words considered nonstandard, such as ain't."

With this in mind, what's the "register" your WHO is used to from their current teachers/mentors/trainers/pastors/coaches (or whoever you are to them)? This especially applies to non-fiction. Your answer to field number two in your book's purpose statement relates to your voice. For example, the way you'd speak and the words you'd choose when you talk to a kindergartner vs. how you'd speak to your college professor would most likely be quite different. Or imagine the difference between how you'd speak as you tell a story to your sister vs. how you'd speak to someone you were counseling.

When it comes to communication (written and spoken), there are five general categories of register: high formal, formal, neutral, informal, and vulgar. Someone in the military would ask (formally), "Permission to speak freely, Commander," and would then be given permission to speak more informally.

A conversation between co-workers might include, "Excuse me, I need to use the restroom for a moment," but a guy might say to his buddy, "Man, I really gotta pee."

Technicians or scientists who know each other well and who are working on a project together might say, "This was a flop and it was a complete waste of our time." Scientists reporting the same incident to the media might say, "The outcome of this experiment was a failure and did not meet our expectations."

Do you notice the difference? The same general message, thought or idea can be communicated in many various ways. That's at least partially what voice is about.

So what register should you use when you write? As you think about it, at least partially, it may also be about your unique personality. For me, my register tends to be more informal and casual, but I can easily alter my register when writing or speaking as appropriate. You can be yourself, but know your audience and know who you want to be to them and it will help you choose.

Let's look at a few of our options for who you want to *be* to your reader and what those types of voices might sound like.

Voices:
Trainer/Coach – motivational, supportive, helpful, positive
Expert – confident, results-oriented, proficient, direct

Technical – factual and usually more formal
Friend – conversational, informal, candid
Pastor/Counselor – with a gentle, yet advisory tone, guidance
Teacher/Educator – practical, instructional, neutral register
Storyteller – whimsical and descriptive, using many stories

To add another layer of your voice, here are some examples of different voice tones you might have, which can pair up with the voice types.

Voice tones:
Sarcastic
Factual
Humorous
Silly
Poetic
Gentle
Powerful/Fiery/Passionate
Dry, Manipulative, Snarky/Jerk (probably best for fiction characters only!)

Imagine how these combinations (tones and voices) could work together:

Humorous storyteller
Humorous coach
Factual coach
Sarcastic friend
Poetic teacher
Silly teacher
Passionate pastor
Passionate expert

When it comes to fiction, your unique author voice will shine through. I remember reading an article by a librarian who was convinced the (at the time) new book *Thinner* by Richard Bachman was really written by Stephen King. She was right, even though it took a while for Stephen King to admit he wrote it under a pen name. Nevertheless, his author voice was distinct and recognizable.

Also, fiction characters even have voices of their own. As you write their dialogue, their voices should stay consistent throughout. If you have one snarky sarcastic character, keep their voice consistently snarky, unless part of the story happens to be their evolution as a person. Genres may even dictate some aspects of voice, as you can imagine the feel and voice differences between horror, romance and young adult books.

If you write a children's book with several characters who are dogs, each dog will have slightly different voices based on their personalities. If you write teen fiction, there may be a harsh queen contrasted by a character who's a gentle, soft-spoken peasant. If you write an action novel, you may have a man who's a high-intensity spy paired with a quirky, witty woman who he is charged to keep out of harm's way. If you write in the historical romance genre, you might have a young, old-fashioned Amish widow who meets and falls in love with a shell-shocked soldier returning from war. When imagining these scenarios, it's easy to understand the need for consistent character voices.

Fiction requires an over-all voice as well. It's more of a consistent "feel" in the book (or series). Will your book have one of these feels to it? Mysterious, energizing, dreary, ominous, uplifting, hopeful, romantic, enchanting, intellectual, etc. When it comes to fiction, also be consistent with your voice throughout when it comes to writing in either first, second or third person, and present or past tense.

Whether you're writing fiction or non-fiction, here's one last thought for now about the voice in your book (until I bring it up one more time in chapter 4): keep your voice consistent throughout. If you change your voice, it will start to seem weird to your reader, but they may not be able to figure out why, exactly.

Organizing Your Content

Now, let's get back on track with organizing all your ideas as you get ready to write. Organizing your ideas well is a big deal. There's a hard way to write a book and an easy way. I've done both, but the easy way is my preference!

The hard way is to throw all kinds of ideas into a document (or in multiple spots), and then attempt to rearrange it at some point later. Ugh, that is arduous. With my first book, that's what happened, but never again since. The easier, more straight-forward way is to start out with being and feeling organized.

For many years I've been teaching a two-step process for organizing your ideas and content. Step one is doing a visual exercise called *book mapping*. Many authors find it helpful to brainstorm and create a visual prior to the detailed structure of an outline. If you take a blank piece of paper, a white board, a mind-mapping app, a napkin or whatever you prefer, you can start to brainstorm main points, major scenes and other ideas for what needs to be included in your book.

You can start with a template similar to this:

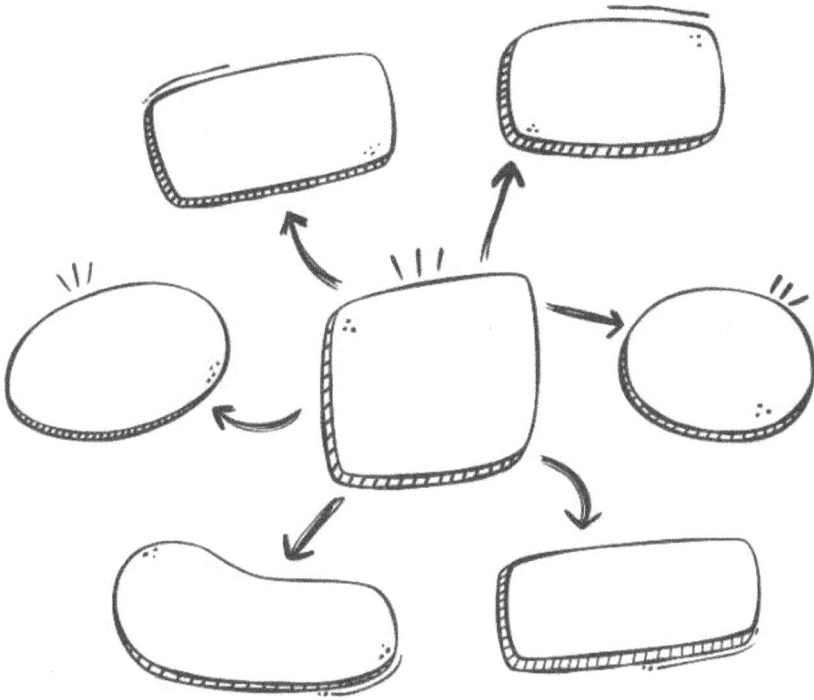

From the major themes, also include any sub-thoughts, ideas and information that belong with that point or scene sequence. To download a blank book map template you can print and use, visit www.internationalpwa.com/freeworksheets now.

Here's an example of what that might look like showing just the major themes:

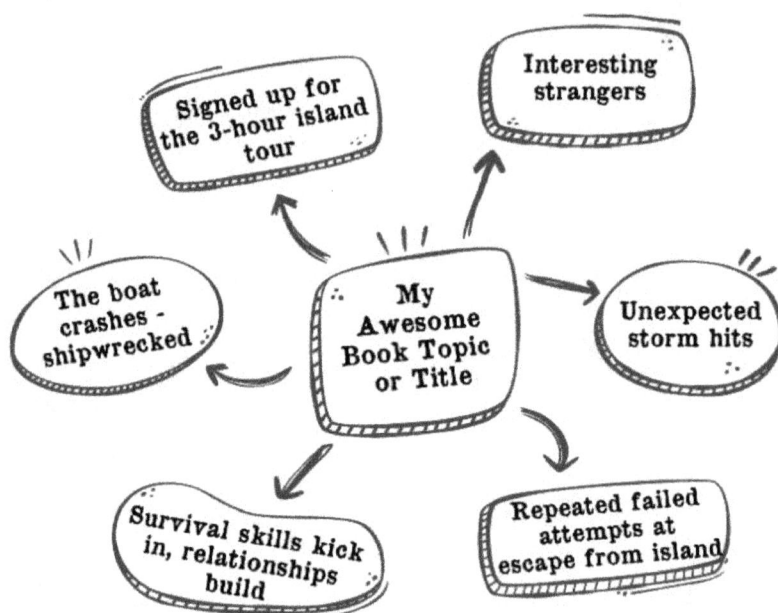

It may take you ten minutes to complete this or several days. Doing this step can be fun and it is certainly helpful. I've known two people who've had various ideas for their books written on many sticky notes and 3"x5" cards; it felt overwhelming. However, when they did this book mapping exercise, it freed them up to be able to put all of their separate ideas all into one place, visually representing the book as a whole. From there, they were more easily able to take the next step and set up an outline with a logical flow of content. Book mapping takes an author from feeling scattered to having greater clarity.

Once you have done some book mapping, you can then take your mapped ideas and start to build an actual outline, becoming chapters and subpoints/scenes. I can't stress enough how powerful this two-step process is. It not only helps you feel more emotionally and mentally settled and clear about your direction, it also helps you write a lot faster. The outlining phase is something I could explain and instruct on for a while, but let me leave you with a couple thoughts.

The order in which your book's content is laid out (the outline) must be logical and carry readers through smoothly from one thought/point to the next. If you're writing non-fiction, consider what your reader must know or understand first. When you reflect on how someone learns and grows, it's like a staircase. Each step builds a foundation, allowing the person to get the information and understanding, facts and revelation they need, and then they can step up to the next level. The most effective books do this too. I'll talk about this thought more in a moment.

Outlines for how-to books are quite easy to figure out; just order it all in the necessary steps your reader needs to take. If you're writing a memoir or some kind of book based on your personal journey or story, chronologically organizing the flow is best. I'll also talk more about this in a moment.

If you're writing fiction, you may want to take one extra step between book mapping and outlining: work on a plot timeline story arc. It maps out the sequence of the book's plot—the scenes, back story, location changes, character introductions, plot twists, action climax, the story's resolution, etc. It helps you put all the scenes in order, in a timeline. With your book map and plot timeline story arc in hand, getting an outline into a Word document (Google Docs or whatever you choose to use while drafting your manuscript) will go quickly.

It's my strong recommendation that you do not skip these book mapping and outlining steps in your book process. Even if you've already written a bunch and are tempted not to do it, reconsider! The way you layout your content's flow is vital. It's easy to copy and paste what you've already written into an amazing, smooth journey for your readers.

Timelines and Steps

To dive deeper into our content organization topic, let me ask you this: are you writing a non-fiction book that has clear steps for readers to take, or does the content follow a chronological timeline? If so, lucky you! These are some of the most straight-forward books to outline and write. There's no *wondering what order to put the content in* because a logical flow of what you need to say is already set. Your timeline or steps sequence is like a backbone for the information, carrying readers through from start to finish.

As you work on outlining your step-by-step book, whether that is a practical topic like business marketing or home renovation, or a spiritual or emotional topic like breaking free from addiction or __xyz__, order your content and steps with two things in mind: what do they need to *understand* first, and then what do they need to *do?* Often people need to have an understanding or awareness of the basics at each step before they can take action on it.

Also, most how-to instructions walk people through logical steps. You have to do this __ before you can do this __. You have to plan your deck's shape and size before you can calculate and buy the materials. You have to understand that God exists before you can understand that He loves you. You have to understand the psychology of colors in branding before you can choose and design your logo.

For memoirs, testimonials, personal journey and other types of books that rely heavily on past experiences and personal stories, I have a couple thoughts. First, sticking to a chronological order of events is best practice. If you've ever watched a movie, heard someone telling a story or read something that skipped around a lot with the timeframes, it can be super confusing. This is what we don't want as authors: confused readers. Fiction authors can get away with some foreshadowing and flashbacks once a foundation and context is set (if they are skilled writers), but for non-fiction books based on life events, it's best to stick to the timeline.

Choose Stories Wisely

If your book will include true stories from your life, is based on your personal testimony, a journey you walked through and/or your life experiences, these types of books are powerful. People love to read about how others have overcome obstacles in life, especially if the person reading is facing the same obstacle right now.

If you have a book like this in your heart now or plan to write one in the future, choose stories from your past strategically and intentionally. We have decades worth of stories, experiences and situations to potentially share, right? But not all of them will apply to every book's message or audience you'll write to. As I write this book now, I'm not including personal stories about my marriage, parenting or finances. I'm not explaining about overcoming timidity or revelations God has shown me over the years. This book has a specific audience: people who want to write books. Here, I'm using only the stories and experiences that apply to you and this topic.

If I'm writing a non-fiction book about how I discovered my life's purpose and calling, including stories about business branding and marketing would not apply at all! If I'm writing a book about my journey as an entrepreneur, my stories about fertility issues have nothing to do with that. All of us have lives full of great stories, but be very selective. Only pull out the stories and situations applicable to the audience and topic you're writing for now. Pick out all the significant events, situations and conversations that relate specifically to this book's message and this reader. Other information may be for another book! (That is, unless you are purposefully writing some kind of very comprehensive autobiography.)

Likewise, think about what stories tie into the theme of each book/message you have. All other stories are for a different time, a different book. If you're writing a book about your past experience with an abusive relationship, chances are you should not include stories about diet, workout and training routines you've practiced since high school. A different audience would care about that aspect of your life. If you're writing about your journey to becoming an artist, who cares about all the pets you've owned in your lifetime? Someone else might, but not the readers interested in your art journey. Even if you're working on a memoir about your life in general, think about the stories you have that tie into the overall feel or theme you want to convey with your book.

Even fiction authors use stories from their own lives and things, situations or people they've observed, so search your past for the perfect experiences to use and describe for each type of book you write. Don't feel the need to tell every detail of your whole life's story. There isn't time and frankly, it isn't all relevant to your book's targeted message/topic. Many of our life stories will be non-essential in certain types of books we may write.

If you are writing a book based on personal experiences, a journey or your testimony, take some time to brainstorm ideal stories and situations to include. List them out, putting them in chronological order, and it will be one more way to help organize your book's flow and content. Fact, fact, fact and more facts doesn't make for very exciting, reader-friendly content for your story, so make sure your stories and experiences go beyond detailing chronological facts in the way you write them.

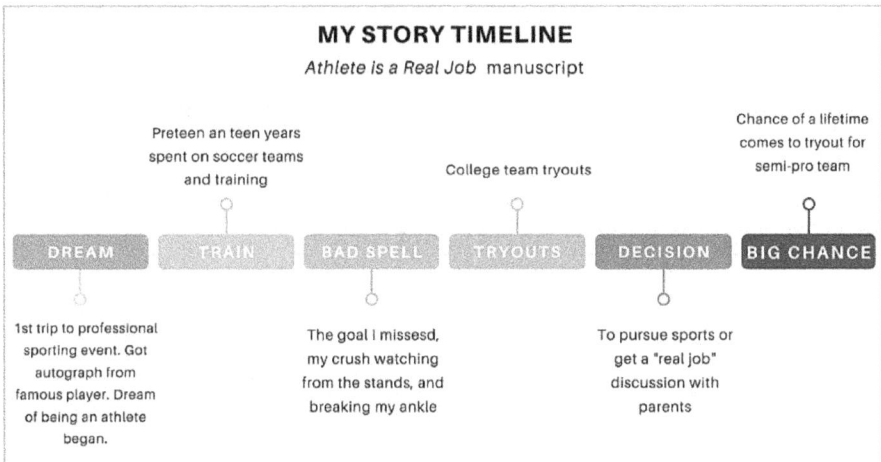

MY STORY TIMELINE

Athlete is a Real Job manuscript

| DREAM | TRAIN | BAD SPELL | TRYOUTS | DECISION | BIG CHANCE |

Preteen an teen years spent on soccer teams and training

College team tryouts

Chance of a lifetime comes to tryout for semi-pro team

1st trip to professional sporting event. Got autograph from famous player. Dream of being an athlete began.

The goal I missesd, my crush watching from the stands, and breaking my ankle

To pursue sports or get a "real job" discussion with parents

If you have a main character for your fiction book who you want to develop out in great detail, especially if this character will be in a series you'll write, you could create a story timeline for their life, giving yourself massive background, flashback, side stories, etc., to work with as you write.

To download a free story timeline worksheet you can use right now, go to www.internationalpwa.com/freeworksheets.

This one last thought for organizing book ideas and content brings me to an online service called Scrivener. According to their website, "Scrivener is the go-to app for writers of all kinds, used every day by best-selling novelists, screenwriters, non-fiction writers, students, academics, lawyers, journalists, translators and more." It is a software program specifically made for authors to help write, organize and arrange content, notes, chapters, research, etc. For authors and writers who don't have a good system of organization for themselves established, Scrivener could be a good option to consider. A link to check out Scrivener is listed in the recommended resources section at the back of the book.

That wraps up this chapter on organizing your content. If you've gone through this process and have set up your outline structure, good job! Your left brain will thank you, and so will your right brain, knowing it now has a structure to run free and create within. Now, on to writing.

Chapter Four:

———————

Get Writing

Once you're sufficiently organized with your book's purpose statement, your resource pile, story timelines and outlines, it's time to get writing! If you have already started writing, wrapping back around to work on the organization pieces will still prove valuable.

Using Word or Google Docs are two of the most popular programs to use for writing a manuscript, and you could do some writing in Scrivener too. In fact, did you know that you can use Word from start to finish? Yes, you could use it to start a file/document where you capture all your ideas, create an outline in it, write and edit your entire manuscript, format and do interior styling for the edited version, and then save two different documents—one for your print book and one for your Kindle eBook.

Let me chase a squirrel for a moment. Notice I said *two different documents* for your print vs. Kindle files. When using Word, your print version file can be used to create your Kindle eBook file, but you cannot use the exact same document. There are most likely several kinds of adjustments you will need to make to your print file in order for it to covert properly into a nice-looking Kindle file during the upload process on Amazon. They will be different files.

Here in this book, I do not have time to talk about all the details of how to adjust a print file so it works for Kindle, nor is trying to explain it with words the best way to help people understand the adjustments that will be necessary. This is the type of live training we tackle in the International Prophetic Writers Association. For now, just realize you can use Word for print and Kindle, but the two files will be formatted a bit differently and will need to be saved as separate files. You can also use a program like Designrr to create your e-versions, or other options like InDesign, Scribus, Draft2Digital, Vellum, Canva, or Calibre.

Discussing formatting and file versions is getting a little ahead of ourselves, so let's get back to our topic of writing a book your readers will love. Typically, the writing phase of your book journey ends up taking the longest. There are a few exceptions of course, like a children's picture book that could take one day to write and four months to wait for your illustrator to complete the images. Or, if you choose to publish your book through a traditional publishing company (more on that soon), waiting for them to complete the publishing process could be the longest timeframe.

The key for this phase is consistency; consistent forward movement, writing regularly. Also, remembering your readers who are waiting to read your work and the important purpose you have for this project will help you stick with it!

Key Tips and Some Pitfalls to Avoid Along the Way

In your writing phase, this is where frustration or lack of motivation can set in if we're not careful. Because I want you to be successful and not give up, let's talk about some especially useful tips, things to keep in mind and a few pitfalls to avoid.

Make Writing a Habit

Aside from retreating to a mountain cabin for a few weeks to get a manuscript written (which does sound quite nice), getting your book written will take creating a new habit of writing. Producing a work of art within a routine doesn't always seem glamorous, but it does seem like that's how it's going to be for most of us. We may feel like we're scraping together time crumbs and squeezing writing into them. But no matter when we find time to write, I feel like our writing time is sanctified, set apart, a sacred time where special things can happen.

If writing a book is something you're serious about, writing it needs to be a priority. We've already talked a bit about setting writing goals. You must give it time in your schedule. Along with making time to write, it's wise to take time to improve your writing skills as well. Remember, time, from what I have seen (and experienced myself), is the biggest factor authors struggle with when it comes to completing their manuscripts. Making writing a habit is essential. Depending on what phase of life you're in right now, time may seem to be working against you. But time is not meant to rule you; you are meant to rule over the time you've been given.

As master of your own destiny, you are not a slave to time; you get to decide and prioritize how you spend it. Besides, we have no idea how much time we have here on Earth. Get that book done soon.

So, Krista, how can I find the time to write? What does your writing schedule look like? I've heard these questions many times over the years. For myself, the message that I burn to tell keeps drawing me back to my manuscript. When it's on my mind and I have a goal set, internal motivation kicks in. I write between other projects during the day, I have my manuscript up on my laptop as my family sits to watch a movie after dinner, I write when I travel and on airplanes, I sometimes write after everyone else goes to bed, etc. At this exact moment, my family just got done eating dinner and everyone disbursed to various rooms. Here I am at my laptop…

Other author friends I know have woken up an hour early for a couple months to write first thing in the morning. Someone else I know travels so much, he was able to write several books in one year while on airplanes. I'm helping another author right now edit their third book for the year. We make time for what's important to us. There are so many options for how setting a writing habit could look, so just find something consistent that works for you.

Write at least a little bit every day, if at all possible, because it keeps it in your routine. You know how hard it is to keep going with exercise and eating right if we aren't consistent with it, right? Writing is much the same. Here are a few practical suggestions for finding time to write:

Write on airplanes.
Write instead of watching TV.
Get up earlier for a season.
Stay up later for a season.
Find time during your lunch hour.
Write in between other tasks, using spare chunks of time.
Write during a road trip (while you're not driving!).
Take an audio recorder on long drives and talk out your content.
Take your manuscript on vacation.
Write in huge time blocks (set aside whole days).
Go on a retreat by yourself to write.
Hire someone to do some of your time-consuming tasks.
Make writing appointments with yourself.
Suspend volunteer and extracurricular activities temporarily.

Postpone other major projects.

I'd like to talk a little more about those last three. Set writing appointments with yourself just like you'd schedule in a call, an appointment or meeting. Your writing is that important! Also, many of us have lots of activities going on in life on top of work, family and home responsibilities. We volunteer at school, church or in our neighborhood and have commitments on teams or with other hobbies. What if you suspended those extra things for a short time to focus on your book? How much extra time would you have then? For some of us, a lot more. And don't feel like you're quitting those things for good. It's just a short season, set aside to focus on something else very important to you.

This goes right along with postponing major projects. Whether it's a remodel, landscaping project, a trip or some other idea that would be a big time commitment, consider delaying it a bit until your writing is done.

Especially if you need your book done quickly, something in your schedule has to give, so what area can give right now?

Get Feedback Early

While helping authors with editing over the years, there have been many times when my eyes have been the only ones that have seen a completed manuscript other than the author's. But what happens when a professional editor gets a manuscript that's never been reviewed by anyone else before? Potentially, a couple not-so-awesome things.

First, editors charge more when a manuscript needs a lot of help. Rightly so, as it will take them more time to work on it. Sometimes, as writers, we have some writing *bad habits*, too, and we don't realize it. Getting some extra eyes on the manuscript early by a supportive reviewer or critique partner (or two) could help us stop our repetitive errors much sooner, before an entire manuscript is written with them. Reviewers can also help you be aware of plot or information gaps or other things that need clarification. Some authors join writer's groups for this very reason; it's a great source of feedback.

Get feedback early. Even if you only have part of a chapter written, that's a perfect time to get some comments about your writing style.

Also, an editor may end up telling the author to make significant changes, re-writes or other content adjustments. For an author excited to get their work out, it can be a tough conversation (and more work, when they thought they were done). This, too, could have been at least partially avoided if the author had sought out comments and opinions from a few trusted people during the writing process.

Reviewers could end up giving feedback like, "I didn't understand what you meant right here…you lost me," or "I wish you would have expanded on this story about…" and other observations along the way that will help an author refine their manuscript sooner.

If you want to have someone check your manuscript out, who should you solicit feedback from? What kind of feedback do you ask for? You always have the option to hire a reviewer. Also, people you know who understand your topic well will be most helpful when it comes to content. If you are wondering about your book's content flow, ask a person who is at least somewhat familiar with your topic to at least review your outline. A couple people in your target audience would hopefully have helpful, general comments or can bring up questions they have along the way. Someone who has great proofreading skills and who may spot some bad writing habits you may have is always beneficial.

With friends and family reviewers though, my suggestion is not asking them to edit (beyond some basic proofreading), but just to review and give you some comments and feedback (unless they happen to have excellent editing skills and experience). If you plan to hire an editor, they will do that for you. Giving your manuscript to too many people for editing can end up changing your voice and message, which most authors find undesirable.

Note: don't show your outline or full manuscript to just anyone. If you have any concern, whatsoever, that a certain individual may try to take your book idea and write their own, obviously, skip showing it to them. You always have the option to hire a professional to do a book review/review edit. This caution goes for illustrators too. A couple friends have told me they've sent their children's book manuscript (in full) to (unscrupulous) artists who never did come through on illustrations for them, only to find out later the artist took their book idea, drew illustrations and made it their own. Sadly, things like this happen from time to time. Thankfully though, these are rare occurrences. Most people are honest and will honor someone else's idea.

An illustrator doesn't necessarily need the wording; they need your detailed, precise description of what you want to see on each page. With my fun *Ninja Kitty: Neighborhood Defender* children's book, I never gave my illustrator the full manuscript/wording. I planned out each page, the wording and what the picture needed to be of, and told him exactly what each scene needed to look like.

Using photos, some rough drawings and detailed descriptions, he and I worked together. I would tell him things like, "For this page, the cat is slinking through the yard. We see her from a side view, and she's heading to the right. There's a wooden fence behind her, separating the neighbor's yard. Behind the fence, you can see the moon peeking through a tree. Here's a photo of the kind of tree and fence I have in mind…"

He was trustworthy, but there was really no reason for him to have the word-for-word manuscript. If you need illustrations or graphics for your book, you might consider doing the same. Now, back to helping your writing process go smoothly.

The Death-Trap of Editing

When it comes to editing, there are two phases: self-editing and professional editing (or some level of getting help from someone else who is skilled). Although very necessary, the process of self-editing can have several types of pitfalls for authors. One of those pitfalls can be taking your previous writing time and using it to edit what you've already written in previous sessions. There's no greater writing time stealer than editing! Instead, when you sit down at your computer and open your manuscript file, do a fast, 5-minute review of what you wrote yesterday (or whenever you last wrote).

Doing this quick review will give you a couple benefits. First, it may spark a continuation of thought to help you pick up where you left off (should you choose to do so). It can help you to mentally get back into the focus and flow of your topic. Also, with fresh eyes, you may spot a few things to quickly fix or adjust. The keyword here is *quickly*.

My best advice is to get the meat out first, then season the meat. Here's what I mean by that. Get all of your ideas and content out first, then go through your own editing process next.

You may be thinking, *I plan to hire an editor, so why should I bother editing it first?* Even if you plan to, always have a process to edit yourself first. You'll save yourself some money, you'll improve your writing skills and you'll get more of your ideas in there rather than more of your editor's modifications.

> *"It is perfectly okay to write garbage – as long as you edit brilliantly."* —C. J. Cherryh

Are you striving for perfection? This can be another editing pitfall for some people. Did you know that having 3-4 errors in your book is still considered perfect? Not that we want errors of course, but sometimes as authors we need to be okay with a small amount of imperfection. You've probably heard this saying: "Done beats perfect." We all hope and strive to put out a great-quality book with few to no errors in word or formatting, right? That's the goal; it's a good goal. Our business or brand may depend on our book looking professional. But if this quest for perfection keeps you from finishing your book or ever publishing it, that's a problem.

But there's a solution for this problem: get help! This is why I recommend getting some help with editing and formatting when needed. If you think about it though, what's the worst thing that can happen? Someone points out an error, and you fix it. Problem solved. If you self-publish, it's easy to make a quick change or an edit to your book.

For example, if you self-publish, have your book for sale on Amazon (plus use them to print copies for yourself) and use Word to format your book's Kindle and/or print version, simply open your Word file, fix the error, resave, then re-upload the updated version to your Amazon KDP author account. Done.

Strange but true, this is another death trap for the editing process: "I don't know everything yet." Join the club; none of us do. Over the years, I've heard people say or have sensed they felt like they couldn't finish their book because they didn't know everything yet about their topic. They don't have the full revelation about something. They weren't the top person in their field on this subject. They aren't an expert-level authority. They don't know everything yet. Well, guess what? Neither do I. Yet, here I am writing to you about writing your book anyway!

I have not written or published every type of book there is in the world. Although with over a decade of being an author and working in this industry and having had the opportunity to assist hundreds of authors, do you think I've learned a few things? Certainly, yes, and I believe what I have to share today will make a positive difference in the lives of others on the same journey. There's always more to learn. Maybe you don't know everything yet, but you know something.

Like me, you are learning new things every day. This will continue for the rest of your life. So, if you don't know everything today, when will you, exactly? Will you ever? Remember my friend, Dolly, who wrote her first book at age 91? Maybe she *did* know everything by then! But I personally don't want to wait that long to share some things, and I suspect you don't either.

Today is the day of impact. Today is the day of action. Have the audacity to share what you DO know right now. As my friend and mentor, Pedro Adao, likes to say, "Can a 5th grader teach a 1st grader?" Of course! Dare to think the wisdom, skills, experience and creativity you have at this step of your journey today can and will help others.

It's okay if you don't know everything yet. Write your book anyway.

How to Self-Edit and Review

At this point, you may be wondering *how do I self-edit*? Over the years, I've developed ten different ways that an author can go back and edit and review their manuscript before calling it "complete." There may be more ways than these ten, but here they are.

1. Proofreading – look for basic errors in spelling, punctuation, etc.
2. Fix any of the common writing errors or bad habits – "that," too many sentences starting with I, overuse of emphasis items, etc.
3. Look for areas to spruce up your descriptive writing.
4. Look for places where you can add more details and information in.
5. Look for spots where you can add in a story that matches your point.
6. Find and fill in any gaps in your plot, sequence or information and look for spots where a better transition is needed.
7. Be sure your voice, tone and tense (past, present, future) are consistent throughout.
8. Look for story braid opportunities.
9. Insert hints about your call-to-action.
10. Identify call-outs.

When authors review and edit their book's manuscript in these ways, it ensures they will send the best possible manuscript to their editor and be the most thorough for their readers.

Let's go over number eight and number ten, which we have not talked about yet. After reading the list, you're probably wondering what a story braid is. Pete Vargas of Advance Your Reach, a public speaking skills company, has a great concept for speakers to use as they craft their talks and messages. I believe we can use it as authors too.

Mostly applicable to non-fiction writing, creating a story braid is an effective way to influence, motivate, guide and/or inspire those who you are communicating to (speaking or writing). Like a braid, there are three elements woven together: heart, head and hands. It's all about putting what you want to say in a certain order.

Heart – first, introduce your topic with a story, fact or observation that touches someone's emotions.
Head – next, give the facts necessary to help the person have greater understanding and detail.
Hands – then, tell them about real solutions and options for what they can do about it or how they can help.
Heart – last, wrap up the message with one more thought to impact their heart.

If you were writing a short lead-magnet book, where you were helping readers (potential customers) understand what you do, your entire book could be in a story braid format. The story braid format would also work well for the last part of a book where you were imploring readers to take action on a cause or embark on a transformative journey.

Here's a short example of a story braid that's a true story. I could either speak this or write this:

What if you, for your entire life, never owned a book? Did you know that in certain parts of the world, families have no books whatsoever? Can you imagine not owning one single book? No bedtime books to read to your children, no school books for learning, no books to learn new skills or ideas. When I was in Ghana, Africa, two years ago, I got a first-hand look at an area of the world where this is a reality. In certain parts of their country, services and opportunities were plentiful. In others, people were just trying to survive, living in shacks that wouldn't even be adequate as a garden shed for us, unable to find work. Some were desperate to find ways to care for their families. *(Heart: grips hearts – in this case, shows the tragedy/injustice.)*

In rural areas of Africa, books are hard to come by. Printing facilities don't exist and libraries may only be found in large cities. Because they are so prized, books are rarely shared or given away. Access to books is access to education. According to GlobalCitizen.org, lack of learning materials is number 4 on the list of the top 10 biggest barriers to education for children around the world. I even read recently that 61% of low-income homes in the US have no children's books. Here in our own country! *(Head: facts, details and explanation.)*

It doesn't have to be this way; we can make a difference. My church, right now, is gathering thousands of books to send to the nation of Ghana in West Africa. We have partnered with several churches in Ghana to create church-based libraries and learning centers in rural areas. Our goal is to fill up a shipping container in the next two months. Do you have books and school supplies you can donate to this cause? Would you like to donate to help pay for shipping the container? *(Hands: call-to-action.)*

I sat next to a Ghanaian man on an airplane as I headed from Amsterdam to Accra, Ghana, for that mission trip. As we talked about his country, he was very proud of it; proud of the natural resources within, proud of the kind, friendly people, proud of the progress they have made in the last decade. "If there's anything we need," he said, "it is more education and information." Here in the US, we take for granted the vast educational and informational resources we have at our fingertips, at local libraries, on television, on the Internet, and in schools and universities. Please support this cause with your book donations, and uplift an entire people group, helping them to gain wisdom, skills and knowledge. *(End with heart again.)*

You can use this braid and wrap technique for main points you're trying to convey and things you're hoping to help your readers understand at a deeper level. If you're someone who tends to speak to heads and logic a lot, really consider changing your writing style up a bit to do this when you want your reader to have a deeper investment in the idea or concept or story. Our hearts are the deeper level we can speak and write to, and it's important to do so. Just don't camp there forever. People still need the information and details to feed our logical side.

When you speak, present or train, use this same technique. We can intentionally use our stories to speak to hearts when we want and need to, and to logic when we want and need to.

Don't worry, it's not manipulation. Fake news is manipulation. Half-truths and spin and propaganda—those are manipulation. Influence can be used for good or evil. When we write books, we are naturally influencing. Was my Ghana story manipulative? No, it wasn't; it was informative and factual. So when we do it the right away, with the right motivation, the person (the listener or reader) ultimately makes the choice to do something with that or not, but they are now touched and informed.

Now, for the last on our editing/reviewing list: call-outs. As you can see on this page and the next, I have created a couple call-outs. They are the power statements or succinct, summarized phrases that authors purposely want to stand out. Formatting call-outs has some options; you can set them apart in a box, by using bold and centering them or with some other formatting style.

Here's a simple call-out formatting style right here:

Call-outs are most commonly used in non-fiction.

Notice how a call-out doesn't necessarily have to be word-for-word how you said it in the main text, but it does need to be a complete sentence in itself.

> *Call-outs are power thoughts, set apart somehow.*

If you want to utilize call-outs in your book, peruse through your manuscript and look for phrases, powerful ideas or deep thoughts you want to emphasize; thoughts you think should stick readers' minds. Again, like the story braid, these are most commonly used in non-fiction books. Check out books currently on your bookshelf to see more examples of how other authors have used them in their books.

Self-editing and review could probably be a whole book in itself. For now, just know that it's a necessary step in your manuscript's progression. If you need to step away from your manuscript for a day or two so you can get some fresh eyes on it for this review and editing process, I completely agree that it could be needed.

Transitions

If you have something valuable to share with your readers, it's important to help them easily follow the flow of your story or information from start to finish. As authors, we want our readers to keep up and see a clear sequence in the book's information. Throughout our book, we are carrying readers from idea to idea, scene to scene, step to step, story to story. Mastering transitions helps us do this well. Not using transitions well (or at all) leaves readers confused.

Here are a few different types of transitions in books:

1. Transition phrases or words to connect sentences, ideas and timelines
2. Transition sentences that connect larger concepts and sections
3. Strategic quotes, scriptures or idea breaks for transitions

Although many more exist in addition to these, examples of transition phrases or words we can use include things like:

Time-based words: next, after that happened, a few months later, then, at the same time, prior to this, shortly thereafter, five minutes later, meanwhile, after a while, before long, ages ago, ages before, during this time, yesterday, etc.

Comparison and showing relationship words: consequently, because of this, however, despite this, even so, likewise, as a result, comparatively, whereas, along with, nevertheless, obviously, also, etc.

<u>Words for steps or sequences:</u> first, initially, then, second, next, after, third, also, lastly, finally, in conclusion, etc.

Here are a few examples of using transition wording within sentences to go from one concept to the next, yet still show the relationship between them (the transition word/phrase is underlined):

The house project was a disaster, despite my best efforts. <u>At the same time,</u> work was going fantastically.

The layoffs started at work. <u>Because of this,</u> I couldn't buy the new car we needed.

<u>First,</u> sugar must be slowly added to the mixture. <u>Next,</u> turn the heat up and boil the mixture for several minutes.

Our city's yearly parade was happening downtown, with great fanfare and commotion. <u>Meanwhile,</u> across town, a silent tragedy was brewing.

His repeated attempts at completing the course failed. <u>Even so,</u> Emily was intrigued by his courage.

As you read through those, notice how your mind correlates how these situations/themes are related or how your mind shifts to a new setting/thought. That's exactly what's supposed to happen!

Lastly, strategically placed/used quotes, scriptures or idea breaks can be very effective as transitions. Here are a couple examples of how you could use those within your book's chapters:

And this is how the post-WWII group originally formed.

"...ask not what your country can do for you – ask what can you do for your country." —President John F. Kennedy

In 1971, when the war in Vietnam was highly protested here in the States, there were several major incidents.

Notice this transition is a quote, centered and italicized, that generally matches the theme of both the paragraphs before and after it. The quote does a good job of separating the two paragraphs, which are on different topics within a chapter. Here's the second idea:

It was the last time I ever doubted him. The outcome was greater than I could have asked for.

Life Is A Gift

The next year was a whirlwind, filled with travel, new friends and a time of redefining my priorities.

Notice this transition is a short thought in bold, creating a separation between the last thought and a new one. If you look closely, you'll see me using all of these types of transitions here in this book.

Transitions help readers make logical connections between ideas, topics, sentences, paragraphs, and shows the flow of events on a timeline. Transitions keep the flow of the discussion going and fill in the thought blanks. They help a reader's mind shift gears. In short, transitions are an author's best friend (for fiction and non-fiction). Use them wisely, and use them often.

Voice

Remember when we talked about how authors should be conscious of what "voice" they're using in their books? This is a reminder to keep your voice in mind as you write. Consistency is key.

Here in this book, I've chosen a friendly teacher voice—part friend, part teacher. Depending on what type of book you're writing and to whom, there's a perfect voice that fits you, the subject matter and the reader.

For fiction, the concept of voice has some different implications. If you are writing fiction, your characters can each have one of these sub-voices, although the over-all voice should be consistent. Whether you choose to write in present or past tense and first, second or third person is also important; keep it the same throughout.

Grammarly defines those *person* options this way:
- First person is the I/we perspective.
- Second person is the you perspective.
- Third person is the he/she/it/they perspective.

Have Community

If you're like me, you enjoy some writing time alone, but being around other creative people sparks ideas and motivation. There's nothing better than finding a group of supportive, encouraging people who are on the same journey as you.

As authors, it's important to keep up with the ever-changing trends and tools. If for no other reason, being around other authors keeps us motivated and more likely to continue moving forward with our writing projects. As you may know, it's too easy to put our book ideas and manuscripts on the backburner. Life happens, and taking our ideas to completion (in this case, to publication) often needs the support of others.

Community is where you find assistance, share ideas, get motivated, offer mutual feedback, get encouragement when you feel stuck, have opportunities to collaborate, find new friends, and more. Local writer's groups may be available in your area, although there are some golden opportunities now for finding writer communities online too.

I'd like to invite you to join us in the International Prophetic Writers Association, where we have a wonderful community of authors working on amazing projects. Get more information now at www.internationalpwa.com. Every author who joins us enhances and enriches our community with their ideas and creativity.

Now that you know multiple methods to employ when writing, let's talk about even more ways to improve your writing skills.

———————————

Chapter Five

Improve Your Skills

Being an author is an ever-evolving endeavor. Our skill level should also be evolving. Typically, we start out our author journey with a story to tell or something to say, but don't really know what we're doing at first. Like any career path or business, we need education and practice in order to get good at it. Strengthen your writing muscle by writing regularly, getting feedback and learning new tricks. It would be almost miraculous for a brand-new writer to write a perfect masterpiece with no instruction their first time out.

Have you ever heard anyone say that new authors should expect their first book to be bad? I'm definitely not saying that's the case, but I've heard author coaches telling people this. I disagree! Sure, your first book will be the one you write when you have the least amount of experience, but expecting it to be bad? No thanks; it doesn't have to be that way.

If you feel like what you've written the first time around is truly sub-par, then call it an experiment where you learned a lot about writing, call it the first draft of your manuscript, call it a work in progress and continue to work on it. You don't have to publish it yet (or ever for that matter), but you don't have to put out something mediocre. Again though, beware of perfectionism's sticky trap. If you're unsure of whether or not what you've written is ready to put out there for all to see, get some reviewers and feedback. More on that in a minute.

In any case, developing our skills and continuing to learn over the years is very valuable as authors. Here are the essential skills for us to continuously be building:

Writing skills
Marketing skills
Learning and keeping up with current publishing processes and programs

Although there are many ways a person can improve their writing skills, for our discussion here, I want to bring up a couple key ideas to help you up your writing game as an author immediately. One is making sure you're avoiding common writing errors, and the other is getting good at writing descriptively. First, let's go over some of the errors I see authors and writers making on a regular basis.

Avoid Common Writing Errors

Although this book is not meant to be an in-depth grammar and punctuation lesson, I'd like to briefly discuss some of the common, repetitive errors I see on authors' manuscripts. Of course, writing errors include misspellings and the like, but that's where spell check comes in. Instead, I'd like to bring up these five issues:

#1 – Too many sentences that begin with "I"
#2 – Double-spacing after end punctuation
#3 – Misplaced quotation marks
#4 – "That"
#5 – Emphasis items – !!!, bold, all caps, quotes

Every single one of these tips will improve your writing skills in general—in your books and in everyday emails, letters, social media posts and more. Are you ready? Here we go…

#1 – Too many sentences that begin with "I"

Be careful about having too many sentences starting with "I" near each other. If you're in a section where you're telling personal stories and observations, especially pay attention to this potential writing misstep. There have been many instances where I've seen authors have every single sentence in a paragraph start with "I." For example:

> I had a bad feeling it was going to be a problem. I brushed the feeling off though, thinking it would be fine. I regretted ignoring that inkling later, once the bill came. I couldn't believe what I was seeing!

Please avoid doing this! If you know you have, it's easy to make some simple adjustments to your sentence structure. Adjusted example:

> I had a bad feeling it was going to be a problem. But thinking it would be fine, I brushed the feeling off. Regrettably, ignoring that inkling bit me later, because once the bill came, I couldn't believe what I was seeing!

This is just one of many options for how a writer could adjust their wording to remedy the habit of having too many "I" sentences. As you can see, the second paragraph looks and feels more sophisticated. The first seemed too rudimentary. Watch out for other words besides "I" as well. Any word repetitively used to start sentences too often will need sentence structure adjustment.

#2 – Double-spacing after end punctuation

Despite what some of us learned way back in typing class, when formatting a book for print, double-spacing causes problems, visually. Like you see here in my book, do a single-space after each sentence's end punctuation. Also, notice the text goes from left margin to the right margin. This is called "justify" (sometimes known as full justify). Because justify formatting of paragraphs can stretch sentences from edge to edge, double-spaces will make large, awkward-looking gaps at times.

I've had authors freak out when they hear this, knowing they have a 45,000-word manuscript with double-spaces between every sentence! Not to worry though, as you can use Word's "find and replace" feature to take care of those pesky double-spaces all at once.

#3 – Misplaced quotation marks

When it comes to using quotation marks, it's almost always correct to encompass the end punctuation of a sentence.

I asked Trisha, "How are you today?"
The flowers had a card that said, "From a secret admirer."
Courtney yelled, "Save the whales!"
Be sure to encompass commas as well, when appropriate, like in these examples:

When people mention the so-called "No Man's Land," I'm not sure it exists.
"I'm happy to be of service," Julie replied.

One of the only times you wouldn't encompass the punctuation is in a situation like this:

What did Chris mean when he said, "It doesn't matter anymore"?

To include the question mark inside the quotes would imply that this original phrase was a question, when it wasn't. We are now questioning her original statement, so the quotes go before.

Here's one more exception:

I thought my password was "123catlady".

If you included the period inside the quotes in this situation, it would indicate the period was part of the password itself, which it is not. Other than exceptions like these last two, watch that your quotation marks encompass punctuation.

#4 – "That"

In my estimation, the word "that" is overused and is sometimes unnecessary. Too many *thats* also starts to be bothersome to readers. It's a filler word, so pay attention to how you're using it as you write. I just got done editing a book from an author who loves *thats*. About 60% of them were unnecessary or used improperly, so they had to be changed or removed.

Here are a few examples of how to (and how not to) use *that*.

I had a friend <u>that</u> used to play golf.
I hit a curb <u>that</u> caused me to lose my shoe.
I guess <u>that</u> he didn't know.

Each of these could be altered to read this way instead:

I had a friend <u>who</u> used to play golf. (People are *whos* not *thats*.)

I hit a curb, causing me to lose my shoe. (There are several variations of how this sentence could read without *that*.)

I guess he didn't know. (This one was just totally unnecessary!)

If you've already written part (or all) of your manuscript and wonder if you have overused or misused *that*, review it to see if any of them can go away. When using Word, there is a "find" feature to quickly search for all of your *thats* to give your manuscript a review. Find out if you tend to overuse it or are using it improperly.

#5 – Emphasis items – !!!, bold, all CAPS, "quote marks"
Nothing says unprofessional writing in books (or anywhere else) like the overuse of emphasis items. If you take a look at books on your bookshelf, you will notice exclamation points, bolded text, all caps and quote marks used very sparingly and strategically. Why? Three reasons: using them is visually noisy to readers, it looks unprofessional and if too many things are emphasized, then none are.

When you drive around any American town the week before the 4th of July, what do you see? Fireworks stands that all say "Discount Fireworks." So, if they're all discount pricing... hmm...then really none of them are. It's the same thing with emphasis items in books.

This is NOT a GOOD "habit" to have for writing **books!!!**

Like sentences that start with "I," I've also seen authors have every sentence in a paragraph end with an exclamation point. If you read the professionally-edited books on your bookshelf, you will never see this. Reserve the use of exclamation points for high-intensity sentences only.

Bold: best used for headers or things like section breaks and nothing else within regular text (for design and styling formatting choices only).

Exclamation points: use sparingly, and only use one!

All caps: use it carefully and hardly ever in regular text, as it gives off a yelling vibe.

Quote marks: don't use quotation marks to randomly emphasize certain words, just because. If you want to do that on social media posts for emphasis, well, fine, do what you must, but never in your book. Where and why to use quotes around words has rules of its own.

To see all ten of the most common writing errors to avoid, visit www.internationalpwa.com/freeworksheets and download the handout.

Descriptive Writing

Want to improve your writing skills in general and help your readers enjoy your books more at the same time? Descriptive writing is one of those opportunities. Learning how to write descriptively is easy, although it takes a bit of practice and requires being intentional about it if it's not your usual style.

As authors, it behooves us to make our writing more interesting and captivating for our readers. We can capture imaginations with the *way* we say things as we write. Sometimes what we're saying isn't boring, but the *way* we're saying it is. Descriptive writing helps our readers to experience the scene with us.

"Description begins in the writer's imagination, but should finish in the reader's." —Stephen King

Non-fiction writers, you may be thinking being good at this skill mostly applies to fiction. If you're working on a fiction novel or children's book, of course, being good at this is vital. In that case, you're often making up situations, making up entire worlds and creating people who don't really exist. Being descriptive is absolutely necessary. If you have a book for young children with elaborate illustrations, the images help paint the picture for readers automatically, but being descriptive is still key. However, non-fiction authors can also greatly benefit from being more descriptive.

Non-fiction books have an inherent challenge: readers may start reading the book, but don't always finish it. Yikes! So, if we want to keep our readers reading until the end, in order to teach and share effectively, we have to be able to capture a person's attention. Just ask a middle school math teacher, right?

Here are some advantages of descriptive writing:

- People will enjoy your book more.
- It keeps readers reading, which is important; we want that!
- Rather than words, words, words, the message and information become vivid pictures in readers' imaginations.
- We remember the story or point they described because it gets stuck in our minds as a picture.

I'd compare descriptive writing to the condiment bar at a burger joint. You wanted the burger; you got the burger. It's what you came for, although all the pickles, lettuce, mayo, ketchup, mustard, onions, relish, special sauce, tomato slices, or whatever else you love to add to it makes it amazing. Give your book that extra oomph readers will appreciate.

What are some ideas on how to write descriptively? Here are a few ideas:

For non-fiction, incorporate stories more. People remember stories, especially when they can picture it. Our minds form pictures and pictures are more easily recalled. Plus, stories are just fun. They add variety. In general, incorporate stories throughout your manuscript whenever you can.

Author and leadership coach, John Maxwell, uses storytelling in some of his books in a strategic way. With every teaching point he has, he tells a story first. Could this work for you? It's an idea to consider if it fits your topic, audience and the purpose for your book. Even Jesus used storytelling a lot—parables to help people get a picture of important concepts.

As I mentioned, another idea is to get good at painting a picture of scenes with your words. Paint a picture that your reader can see in their mind. Can they see it and picture themselves there? Can they experience it too, in a way? Here's how we can do that:

Vividly describe scenes and surroundings using the five senses: sight, sound, smell, touch/feel, and taste. Give information that caters to these senses and helps readers to experience the scene for themselves.

The beach was hot and sandy, and the water felt good on my toes.

Well, this description is super basic. We got meat and a bun. A nice, clear picture of this scene doesn't form in our minds though. What about this description instead?

The cove's secluded, white sand beach was a dream. Heat radiated off the powdery sand, causing the need to tiptoe quickly across with our bare feet to reach the cool, turquoise waves gently lapping in.

This one is much better, giving us a tropical picture of paradise!

Description Gone Wild

Now that I've encouraged you to be descriptive, I have one warning: don't go crazy with elaborate descriptions of absolutely everything you mention. When writer's do this, it can get annoying, distracting and cumbersome.

Before lunchtime, I decided to take a half-a-mile walk in the sweltering, noonday sun to my best friend's house. With my trusty, worn canteen in hand, I set off down our gravel driveway towards Persnickity Avenue, the main road in town. Our field grass along the driveway was brown, dry and tall—up to my ribs. It waved in the light breeze, reminding me I hadn't finished mowing yesterday, and so did the old, green John Deer mower sitting off to the right about 15 feet away. Rounding the corner at the end of the driveway, heading north, I avoided stepping into the gaping hole my dad dug last week for the cedar post that will house our new, bright yellow mailbox still not installed. The dusty, roadside blackberry bushes were in full bloom. Bees and flies flitted from flower to flower, expertly missing the vines' thick thorns. The brambles intertwined with a rusty chain-link fence with two layers of thin, silver razor wire clumsily adorning the top. The cracked cement sidewalk had a steady stream of redheaded ants marching in a line, making their way to who-knows-where. Several vines tumbled across the sidewalk along my path, catching twice on my knee-high, white tube socks with three red stripes. A black crow cawed loudly, drawing my attention upward where I noticed Mr. Smith's extra-long flagpole flying two large flags: a ragged, wind-tattered stars and stripes and a black, skull and crossbones pirate flag.

At some point, you probably zoned out and stopped reading that paragraph! If so, I don't blame you. It was extremely descriptive, over-the-top wordy and may have taken too much effort to sift through. And did that scene really warrant such detail?

If you were to write about picking up a pen to sign a document, there's no need to go into great detail about the pen's look and feel (unless it happens to have important, symbolic meaning).

If you're writing about driving by a beautiful field with cows, there's no need to describe every cow. It's just too much.

If you're writing about getting ready in the morning and going out your front door and it takes five paragraphs of unnecessary description about what your shoes look like, how you did your hair and which styling tools you used, which color/style/fabric coat you put on, details about all the mess in the hallway, what you ate for breakfast and how much, and the style of doorknob you have as you turn it to go out the door, that's probably way too much!

Don't go wild with descriptive writing, but learn to use it strategically to set the important scenes. There are ways to use it lightly often. Get very descriptive only with portions of stories and scenes that are significant.

Description Has Perspective

Think about this: when it comes to descriptions, *who* is describing it also matters. The mindset or perspective of the person observing the scene (when describing a true story or if it's a fiction character) sets the tone for descriptions. What do I mean? Examples:

Someone feeling depressed: *Glancing around, while standing in the doorway, the half-empty room seemed drab and tired. Thick dust lined the fireplace mantel, along with random, unmatching photo frames filled with yesteryear's faded memories. Here and there, a few furniture pieces covered with old, ugly sheets sat motionless.*

Someone feeling fearful: *The cavernous room had an unsettling feel and gave no invitation for comfort. Like ghostly figures, dingy, white sheets covered some pieces of furniture scattered throughout the room. Frozen in time like a crime scene, this forgotten space hadn't seen life in years.*

Someone who is bored: *Walking through the doorway, as if hoping to discover a new scene, the lifeless room looked to be frozen in time. A few pieces of furniture sat covered, old pictures donned the mantel and even the spiders had long-since abandoned their stringy webs hanging in the corner. It was the same uninteresting space, day after day, offering no opportunity for amusement.*

Someone who is curious: *The room was a blank slate, a playground for the curious. What's under the sheets? Who are these people in the photos? Why is this room not being used? Who painted this masterpiece leaning against the wall in the corner? The abandoned living room contained more questions than answers.*

Someone who is young: *Rounding the corner of the arched doorway, she stopped to take in the scene. A large, partially-empty living room was before her, with plenty of room to run and new things to be explored. Wanting to take a peek, she discovered old furniture was hidden underneath the old, dusty sheets spread around the room.*

Someone who is grieving: *The old, unused living room, in its current state, seemed sad and forgotten. Away from a few other furniture pieces, one lone chair sat off to the side near the fireplace, covered in an old, white sheet. Seeing the old photos of happier days arranged on the stone fireplace's mantel caused a sting of emotion. Heading across the worn carpet, I wanted to get a closer look. Plucking one frame from the mantel, I dusted it off and examined it closely for several minutes.*

This could be the exact same location with all of these people, right? But their perspective and frame of mind is the way they're seeing it. As you noticed, each one is vastly different, depending on who's looking. Not every scene you may need to describe has a lot of emotion in it, however, but when it does, use it.

Remember, just as we describe details about the physical surroundings, we can also describe our internal environment (or our characters') as well. Our internal environment includes things like our thoughts, reactions, emotions, assumptions, attitudes, and feelings. We even can talk about and describe our sixth sense, things like gut reactions, the knowing in our spirits and the feelings that something is or isn't right.

Alarms were going off in my mind; there was a knot forming in my stomach. In my spirit I knew something was wrong.

Idioms and Comparisons

Here are a couple more fun ideas for upping your descriptive writing game: idioms and comparisons.

Idioms are expressions that don't mean exactly what their words indicate. They usually have a figurative, sarcastic or metaphorical meaning that brings up a mental picture, despite the combination of words used in the phrase. You've most likely heard these idioms before:

He was like a bull in a China shop.
It's raining cats and dogs.
It hit me like a ton of bricks.
I've got butterflies in my stomach.
Don't make a mountain out of a molehill.
If the shoe fits, wear it.
She was barking up the wrong tree.
Give them a taste of their own medicine.
He was feeling under the weather.

If she was *barking up the wrong tree*, chances are good she was never actually barking, nor was there a nearby tree involved! This saying means she was looking, asking or trying to get answers from the wrong source. Idioms can be a good way to say things more creatively as you write, allowing your readers to get mental images to *see* what you're saying.

Idioms already exist in various languages and cultures, with some new ones created now and then, but comparisons are something you can make up yourself, as needed. Check out these examples of comparisons:

The massage melted my stress away like butter.
She was like a lamb in a wolves' den.
The event was like a three-ring circus with no ringmaster.
The answer came like a long, winding road.
The city looked like a busy beehive in spring.
His breath was like a port-o-potty in mid-July.

Comparisons are fun and can be a useful tool for writers. Hopefully now you have a greater picture of the importance of stories, descriptions and a few other ways to spice up your writing so your points get across and readers keep reading.

I hope those tips have given you new ideas for how to become a better writer. Now, onto a tip that will help improve your marketing skills; something to consider even before your book is published.

Your Call-to-Action and Reader Next Steps

As an author, how can you continue the conversation with your readers? If you were wondering if this is even important, yes, it very much is! During our discussion about writing your book's purpose statement I mentioned this concept of having a call-to-action. Let's talk about it again.

Imagine a reader who picks your book up and reads it cover to cover. After doing so, they've gotten to know you (non-fiction) or your storytelling style (fiction). If they like what they read, chances are they're going to want more from you. What do you have to offer them?

Have you ever been to a conference or event where the speaker sold their books at the back of the room after their session? Me too. In fact, I've been that speaker before! Now it's your turn. Speakers have figured something out. They want to continue the conversation with the audience long after they've stepped off the stage and gone home.

Some speakers and other authors, however, do something with their books that is even smarter. Not only do they sell books to help the conversation (and their influence) to continue, but their book(s) also contains another call-to-action inside.

What is a call-to-action? It's specific direction and/or an opportunity given to readers for next steps they can take with the author. For an author, it's more ways for their influence, services, other books and/or message to continue impacting readers; ways for readers to stay connected to them and vice versa. You can do this too.

Here are some call-to-action examples you could consider including in your book:

A link to sign up for your e-newsletter
Information and links to your YouTube channel
A link to your blog or podcast
How readers can access a free report you've created
Contact you about speaking at their event or meeting
How to order other books you've written
How to join a challenge or class you have
To follow you on Instagram

Join a Facebook group you run
Request a 20-minute free consultation with you

There's so much more to know about call-to-action opportunities and how to take advantage of them as an author. In fact, this is directly related to book marketing and business strategy, and it could be a long book of its own. For now, I hope this gets you thinking beyond just your book's content and what else you could offer to help your readers. If you look closely, you'll even see some call-to-actions here in this book.

As authors, improving our writing, publishing and marketing skills is a journey we all take; a very worthwhile and rewarding journey. Who do you have that is on this journey with you? Do you have a community or place of learning where you can continuously hone your craft? I hope so, because community will help ensure your growth as an author and makes it more likely that you'll finish and publish your books.

Next, let's talk more about finding the help you may need as an author, including your publishing options.

Chapter Six:

How to Find Publishing Help and Community

Twenty-five years ago, options for getting a book published were fairly limited. But no longer! An explosion of self-publishing options has turned the publishing world upside down, giving authors more control and greater flexibility. With all the options authors have now though, there are pros and cons for each that are important to consider. Each option has some great advantages and some less desirable aspects.

In essence, there are three main options for how you could publish your book today. They are:

1. Get accepted and published by a traditional publisher/publishing house
2. Pure self-publishing
3. Self-publish with some help (hybrid publishing service for hire)

Let's talk about these three in detail for a few minutes to see which route may be best for you and your goals as an author.

Traditional

First, traditional publishing companies like Random House, Simon & Schuster, Thomas Nelson, Scholastic, and HarperCollins have been household names for decades. In my estimation, the pros and benefits of being published by a traditional publisher include things like getting a quality book at the end because they know what they're doing. They have teams of experienced people who've done this work for a long time. It's almost guaranteed they'll do a good job with covers, graphics, editing, formatting, etc. And because they have teams of people working on it, that means you aren't! You write the manuscript and they take over, doing all the work to complete it.

There's also the fact that traditional publishers have closer relationships with bookstores and marketing outlets. Your book may have a greater reach because of their connections and marketing help. However, don't expect they'll be actively marketing your book forever. Your book will get some attention and help at the beginning, but then they'll be onto the next launch shortly thereafter.

The last major pro I can think of is there's a general *cool factor* to say you've been published by a traditional publishing house. It's definitely an accomplishment the masses have not achieved. And if you're wondering about author advances ($$), that still happens sometimes.

From what I've seen, the cons or negatives about this route are three main things. First, it's hard to get a manuscript accepted by a traditional publishing company as a new author. Unless you're famous or infamous, good luck pitching your manuscript and getting easily accepted, especially on your own without a literary agent. It's certainly not impossible, but it's a longshot in many cases and could take a long time.

Yesterday, I read a blog post by an author who decided to self-publish and rely heavily on creating audiobooks after getting 124 rejection letters from traditional publishing companies. After his audiobooks became very popular, suddenly they wanted him after all. Years ago, I had a conversation with Jack Canfield (*Chicken Soup for the Soul* series) where he told me about his original 140+ rejections from publishers. I'm sure all 140+ regretted it later. But anyway...

Second, traditional publishing companies are slow. If you're someone who needs a book produced quickly, either because of a timely story or topic, or your book project is somehow related to your business, ministry or work, keep in mind that it could take a year or more to finally get it in your hands.

Lastly, as an author, you have less control over and "say" about how your book turns out. Once a traditional publisher accepts your manuscript, they take it over. If they don't like your title, they'll change it. If they don't like chapter three, they'll remove it. If they have a different vision for the voice style in the book, they'll edit it to sound less like you. If they don't want to create an audiobook version, they won't (and may or may not allow you to, either). So, as you can see, pros and cons.

Self-Publishing

The next option you have for publishing your book is pure self-publishing. FYI, self-publishing is actually a term for any form of publishing a book without going through a traditional publisher. For our discussion here though, pure self-publishing means you are taking on the whole process yourself. You are the editor, you create the book cover design, you format and do the interior styling to get your book ready for print, you create the Kindle version file, etc. You execute and manage the whole project.

The best thing about this option is that you'll have full control over everything. If you need the book out in two months, if you know what you're doing, no problem. Your timeline goes. You set the retail prices. You control how it's edited. In the end, your book will be exactly how you want it.

Not only do you have full control, but you may save money with this option. Chances are there will still be a few expenses along the way, but pure self-publishing is usually a very affordable way to publish a book on a shoe-string budget. If you want or need to, you could hire help for certain pieces of your project.

There are a few things to seriously consider about this option, however. Two big cons come with pure self-publishing: the time factor and skill/know-how. First, tackling all the publishing-related tasks takes time. The learning curve can be steep for new authors trying to navigate the publishing process on their own. Some people have more money than time, so it still could be an option for them to consider.

Second, for those who don't quite know what they're doing, an important question remains: will the book be the best it can be without having expert help and guidance? If someone does everything themselves, will their book be the best it can be?

With my first book, I didn't know what I didn't know. What I *did* know was that I wanted my book to be good quality when it was done. I also needed to have a greater understanding of how the whole process of publishing worked. So, what did I do? I paid $10,000 (plus travel expenses for multiple trips) for an author coaching program, another $4,000 for a self-publishing/hybrid publishing company (more on that in a moment) to publish my book and another $4,000+ to buy 500 copies of my book. Overkill, you say? Probably, but boy, did I learn a lot through that process. All those experiences (and expenses) set me up to be where I'm at today—helping and training authors—although it never crossed my mind at the time.

Since then, I've published eight more of my books through my own publishing companies. Not that I recommend or think it's necessary to spend $10,000+ for the knowledge you need (nor does every book warrant a $4,000 price tag to publish), as there are now more affordable ways to learn and grow your skills as an author, but getting the knowledge and skills for yourself is key. Just because a lot of people have done it, doesn't mean everyone has done it well. Get the skills and information you need to do it well.

Hybrid

Now it's time to review the pros and cons of the third publishing option authors have: hybrid/pay-for-service/vanity press publishing companies. These are companies that specialize in helping authors with taking their manuscript to print, assisting with all the publishing-related tasks. I've heard a few author coaches, agents and publishing websites criticize companies who offer paid publishing services. Some imply that these companies are scams for authors. Why? It's ridiculous to assume every author will be accepted by a traditional publishing company or that a traditional publisher would be their first and only choice for getting a book out. They serve a great need and gap in the publishing market.

From what I've experienced (and many others), hiring a hybrid publishing company has some benefits. For one, you can hand over your manuscript to them and get a finished book in your hand back. Like traditional publishers, it saves you time. Someone else is doing all the work of publishing for you. Along with that, you don't have to know everything or have all the necessary skills yourself. You're using someone else's expertise. It can sure be nice to have someone who can answer your questions along the way. Some hybrid companies will provide a la carte publishing services if requested.

In addition, unlike traditional publishers, you will have more control over your book. You tell the designer what you'd like to see on your cover, you choose your book's title, and no one is going to arbitrarily remove chapter three! Because not all of these companies are the same, your level of control may vary.

Let's talk about that and some of the less awesome factors of this choice. Obviously, this option costs money. You are paying one of these companies to complete all the publishing steps and produce your book. Costs vary from company to company and sometimes from project to project (because size and scope of each book can be different). Typical pricing will fall somewhere between $2500-$5000 for a full publishing package, which may or may not include any marketing services.

Because the way each company does business varies widely, ask a lot of questions before deciding which pay-for-service publishing company to use. Here are just a few questions I can think of:

Where will my book be listed for sale online?
Do I have full control of my book on Amazon or do you?
Can I find my own source for printing?
Will I get to set my book's retail price?
What kind/level of editing do you typically do?

Do you have editors who are familiar with my genre?

How long will it take for my book to be published?

What will you need me to do during the publishing process?

If I need to add something in or make a change after it's been edited, will that have additional fees?

How in-depth is the design for the cover?

What program do you use to format my interior for print?

Will it be possible for me to edit my interior file myself in the future, if needed?

Do you offer any marketing services with my publishing package?

Will I be able to get the finalized interior and cover files?

Like traditional publishers, many hybrid publishing companies keep an author's book in their company's account on Amazon and with other distribution services and also control the book ordering/printing process (when an author wants to buy copies of their own book). This is starting to change a bit, and a few companies will simply allow authors to create their own author account at kdp.amazon.com and/or IngramSpark so they'll have full control of their own book ordering, online sales royalties, future book updates/adjustments, etc. If the company keeps it in their account, expect there to be a markup on per-copy printing costs and some of the royalty money from online copies sold to be kept by the company.

I can't say my experience with the company I chose to work with for my first book left me 100% satisfied. Knowing what I know now, in my opinion, they price gouge authors, which I don't appreciate and vowed not to do when I started working with authors. They implied marketing services, but come to find out any marketing services they offered were all add-on charges. They only edited one chapter of my 20-chapter book. And like I just mentioned, they kept my book in their accounts adding massive markups when I wanted to order copies of my own book and kept much of my online royalties for themselves. Mind you, this is after paying nearly $4,000 for their services. Chalk it up to life lessons learned, I guess.

Again, pros and cons exist for those situations—you having ordering and online control vs. a company doing it for you—so it just depends on whether or not you'd like their continued involvement or not. In most cases, you probably don't need it.

Thankfully, not all hybrid publishing companies do business the way mine did with my first book. But this is an example of why it's smart to ask a lot of questions up front, and it's a good thing you know what questions to ask now.

"Amazon and Kindle has created the number one opportunity for authors since the dawn of the printing press. Now, the power has been taken from the hands of the publishers and handed into the hands of the authors." —Adam Houge

After reading through your publishing options, which do you think will work best for you? In my humble opinion, it's awesome to be published by a traditional publisher, it's awesome to have a pay-for-service publishing company help you get your book out, and it's awesome to self-publish. When you have your book in your hand, it is amazing no matter which route you took!

Book Formats

We've talked a lot so far about getting your book "published." When many people hear that term, they immediately think of holding a paperback book in their hand. While a print version is the traditional format for books, there are more options for us today. Here are the big three; the most popular book formats now are:

Print   eBook   Audiobook

If you can publish your book in all three formats, do it. If you can only do two formats, do print and eBook (Kindle). If you can only do one, do Kindle (especially if you're writing fiction, although do print if you're a speaker who needs to sell books at the back of the room). Certain readers are very dedicated to their favorite book format, so that's why having your book available in all of them is best, if possible.

For example, a person with a long commute to work Monday through Friday may only buy audiobooks because listening in the car is all they have time for. Some readers love the feel of a real book in their hands and don't care for e-versions. Because eBooks usually cost less than print versions, Kindle fans may snap up several books a month. There are some writers who've decided only to create Kindle eBooks, focusing exclusively on that market. Last week, I told my author group that I'd just done a bit of research in Amazon's Kindle Store and discovered 46 of the 50 top-selling Kindle books were fiction that day!

Apple Books, Kobo, Barnes and Noble and a few other smaller companies are also into the eBook market, but Amazon's Kindle outranks them all in the U.S. for sales volume.

Audiobooks are rising in popularity—faster than the other formats. Today, Audible.com is the most popular site (also connected to Amazon) for buying audiobooks. For general information on audiobooks and to learn how to create an audio version of your book, visit the Audiobook Creation Exchange's website acx.com.

Now that you know the book types you can create and the various publishing options, you have a lot to think about. It's great to have options, and I know there will be one perfect for you right now.

Once you have written your book and published it, then comes the multifaceted task of marketing and selling it. It must get out to your target readers, but how?

_____

Chapter Seven:

Marketing Tools

I know a few people who are great at marketing, but find it difficult to complete their manuscripts. I know many people who complete their manuscripts and get their books published, but aren't great at marketing. Being good at writing does not mean you are good at marketing or vice versa. Either way, most people need some help with certain parts of their book journey. Writing a book is an amazing feat; marketing a book well is another feat in itself!

Remember, as an author, you don't want your book to be like the isolated house in the desert. With marketing efforts, all roads need to lead potential readers right to your book.

"If you aren't a major public figure, it's unrealistic to think you can publish your book and the world will just stumble upon it."
—IngramSpark

How to market and promote a book can sometimes seem elusive. Authors often ask for marketing advice. How (and where) you market your book very much depends on your book's topic and audience. In my opinion, a book's marketing plan needs to be customized, depending on who you're marketing to. It only makes sense, right? Especially when you consider how different a children's picture book for preschoolers, a non-fiction book for Baby Boomers who want to start a business in retirement and a crime and mystery fiction novel are. Book marketing is not one-size-fits-all, but there are some basic things every author can do.

The Marketing Basics

My author marketing advice here is in no way comprehensive, although it will give you a foundation to build upon. Since having a book and being an author is a mini-business in itself, the bare-bones, must-have marketing tools are pretty much the same as any business needs: website, social media presence, email list and/or online community. The key is that all of these need to direct interested people to one main hub, which is usually the author's website. Let's talk about that first.

Website

If you're like a lot of people, you investigate things, people, products and businesses online. My husband is a master researcher who loves to grab his laptop, sit on the couch and investigate before buying something. If he can't find the information he wants, he may not buy anything. He also may not believe the person, business or product is even legit if he can't find it online. I suspect he isn't the only one!

As an author, having a website of some kind is a good idea. It's a great place to let people know more about you, talk about your book(s) and tell people how they can purchase a copy, give people a way to contact you if needed, add information about upcoming events or speaking engagements you have, do some blogging, display some reader testimonials, and more.

To get a website, you'll have to purchase a domain name plus a hosting account. A hosting account is where your site is actually built and lives online. Your domain name and hosting account will need to be renewed each year. There are also a few sites like Wix and Weebly that provide packages to help people easily make websites.

Funnels?

Have you heard of marketing funnels? They are webpages that route potential buyers through a series of steps, information and pages to click through, eventually bringing the site visitor to a purchase now or sign up now spot (depending on the purpose of the funnel). They are designed and meant to turn prospects into buyers (products and services) or interested people into participants (free classes and e-newsletters). Your book's website could actually be a funnel. These days, funnels can be made to look more like regular websites and can contain a good amount of content, images, videos and more.

A funnel will have whatever domain name you choose, just like a regular website. As a side note, I recommend purchasing your name as a domain name, e.g., KristaDunk.com. By having YourName.com, you can give information for as many books as you may write in the future, plus your speaking schedule, reader testimonials, other services you may offer, etc. It's very flexible.

Companies like ClickFunnels, Kartra, Leadpages and others have automated funnels, making it easy for entrepreneurs, authors, speakers, coaches, trainers, people who sell physical products, local businesses, etc., to make sales pages for their products and services. Many funnels people create include a cart/checkout process. These funnel service companies have monthly or yearly fees for anyone who wants an account to create and host funnels online.

Whether you decide to use a funnel service or to set up a more traditional website with a products page where your books are made available for purchase, connect everything marketing-related you do to this spot. Have an active Twitter account?

Regularly include your website link. Have a newsletter list? Be sure to always highlight your website/funnel link. Making business cards for yourself? Add your link. Making an email auto signature? Add your link. Got an author page created for yourself on Facebook? Be sure your link is there. Posting a picture of your book cover on Instagram? Be sure to include your website link for people to click. You get the idea.

Some authors make the decision to direct all buyer traffic directly to Amazon or a different online book-selling site rather than fulfilling customer purchases themselves. You could certainly do this; it makes things easy, although you'll have no idea who buys your book. Amazon will not share customer data with you. If you want to continue the conversation with your readers, this is where having well thought out call-to-actions are a must.

Social Media

My number one recommendation for taking advantage of social media as an author is to have accounts/profiles in the places where your target readers are. Right now, Generation X and Baby Boomers love Facebook. Millennials love Instagram and Pinterest. Business people are typically on LinkedIn. Teens use SnapChat, Instagram and TikTok a lot. Generation X and under are surfing YouTube almost every day, and Boomers are too when the need strikes. Approximately two-thirds of all Twitter accounts belong to men, approximately two-thirds are between the ages of 19-49, and it tends to be a place for political topics, social justice, international themes, micro-blogging, and news.

Sean Cannell, a YouTube expert and owner of Think Media, shares the information below with his community of YouTubers when it comes to how to promote their YouTube channels on social media.

I believe his thoughts about the various social media platforms are also helpful for authors promoting their books.

"With over 500 million users, Instagram is one of the most popular social media platforms for creators and influencers who want to promote their content and connect with their niche.

Instagram, generally thought to best accommodate visually interesting posts, actually gives you a ton of ways to grow your brand and produce a variety of content. You can post photos and short videos on your feed and post photos, videos, and raw footage to your stories to connect with your audience. You can also directly communicate with your followers using polls, Instagram LIVE, and easy-to-use direct messages.

Facebook is a tried-and-true social media platform with over 1 billion active users and amazing marketing opportunities. Facebook Ads is one of the most popular paid advertising opportunities because of how targeted and specific you can make sure your promotions.

Your Facebook posts can include text, photos, and videos and you can also create a separate business or fan page without creating a new Facebook account. There are also many networking opportunities with groups and pages spanning every niche in various parts of the world.

LinkedIn is one of the fastest growing social media platforms with incredible opportunities for organic growth. This is a fantastic platform to be on if your niche is more professional and high ticket. Plus, you can connect your LinkedIn directly to your YouTube channel to promote your videos directly.

You can create text, photo and short video posts on LinkedIn and find other creators easily who are in your niche. LinkedIn also allows you to use hashtags to create more targeted content and reach people who will get the most value from your post."

In a few years, the popular social media platforms will evolve and new ones will emerge. Your job is to stick with the ones you'll actually use and the ones where your target readers frequent. Every time you talk about your books on social media, which you should not do 100% of the time, by the way, direct people back to your main website (or ordering page).

Online and offline, you never know where someone may hear about you or connect with you first. Will they see a post or ad on Facebook? Will they hear about your book because of a Twitter post? Will they see your profile on LinkedIn first? Will they see a YouTube video of you being interviewed? Will they see your book cover image on Pinterest? Will they find your blog or podcast? Will they follow you on Instagram? Will they hear you speak at a local event? Will they see an article about you in a newspaper? Will a friend mention your book to them? Will they meet you at a conference or event? In any case, all roads should lead them back to your site.

Because I mentioned online communities as a marketing basic, I'll briefly discuss that here in the social media area. Since online communities are often set up within social media sites, especially Facebook, technically they'd be part of your social media strategy as an author. You could create communities of your own like we talked about in the building a platform section, or you could join and participate in other groups and communities other people have formed already. I would do both.

Normally, these groups and communities are gathered because they have common interests—sewing, homeschooling, sci-fi enthusiasts, business owners, musicians, youth groups, etc. Take advantage of the many groups out there filled with your target market. Be aware of group rules though, and try not to be spammy about your book all the time. Be social! If it's a community/group you create, bring valuable content, but you can talk about your book as much as you want. Just don't make it 100% book, book, book, or the group members may tire of it.

Email List

As with any business, having an email list of clients, leads and people interested in what you're up to is a huge asset. Most people still do read their emails, and it's an inexpensive way to stay in contact with your reader community. Your list members may be people who have read your book, clients, leads and anyone else who wants to hear about your message or projects. If they've given you their email address, give them valuable information and wisdom with every message you send. Salesy emails all the time gets old, fast. You can also give them something of value for initially signing up for your email list.

Many authors and business people offer a freebie of some kind to anyone who signs up for their email list/e-newsletter. This is sometimes referred to as a lead magnet. There are so many ideas, but a few are that could work well for authors:

A free chapter (or a "bonus" chapter) to read
A report, checklist or tips sheet
A webinar to watch
A special interview, training or broadcast
A downloadable printable item
A short story

You can get away with sending emails through your regular email and using the bcc function (so people can't see each other's emails and don't reply all) if you only have a few dozen people on your email list, but once you get past a few dozen, an email list service of some kind makes sense. Otherwise, your email provider may start to think you're sending out spam messages (plus it gets cumbersome).

MailChimp, Constant Contact, HubSpot and GetResponse are just a few examples of the many email marketing and email list services available for authors and business people to manage their lists and marketing emails. I use Kartra for my websites, funnels, membership area plus its built-in email list service; it's fantastic! There are also services to use for texting your clients and leads. In either case, people need to opt-in to receive these kinds of notifications and emails from you. If you have a website, funnel or social media page, you can put a link up where people can opt-in to your email list and/or text notifications. The link connects directly to your chosen email marketing account.

What if you don't have an email list and aren't sure how to build one? Here are a couple suggestions: either get some training on the best strategies and ideas for how to build your list well and quickly (or hire someone to do it), or leverage the power of the relationships you have with people who already have email lists of your target readers. The best idea is probably to do both.

Many people who have an email list create a weekly, bi-weekly, monthly newsletter of some kind to send out to their list. In order to do this effectively, give your e-newsletter a name, schedule a certain day to create content for it and set up its template, be consistent with how often you send it (per whatever frequency schedule you have decided on) and be sure to offer a lot of value with it every single time it's sent. You can certainly add information in about discounts, special offers, your upcoming events, affiliate links, or other marketing type information, but people want to hear from you with information, inspiration and wisdom *they can use* now. What's in it for me (WIIFM) is why they want to be on your list. Your job is to always consider this: *what's in my newsletter for them?*

More Ideas

There are hundreds more marketing ideas authors could employ to increase book sales and notoriety, but there are a couple worth highlighting here. Specifically, I'd like to talk about podcasting, getting interviews, book reviewers and organizing a launch team.

Podcasting

Hosting a podcast has become hugely popular and available to most anyone who has a few pieces of audio-recording equipment. Several of my friends and business partners host podcasts, each with a different topic and audience. As an author, hosting your own podcast can be an interesting tool, and getting interviews on other people's podcasts is very useful as well.

As of right now (and this changes rapidly), some of the most popular places for podcasters to offer their podcasts are online sites such as iTunes, SoundCloud, Libsyn, PodBean, Spotify, and

Simplecast. I have one friend who records himself with audio and video simultaneously, and uploads the audio for his podcast and uses the video for his YouTube channel. Another friend records his podcast and uploads it to several podcasting sites, rather than just one.

Podcasts are a way for people to get to know you. Listeners can play your recorded podcast episodes any time they'd like, hearing your thoughts, presentations, trainings, opinions, interviews, or whatever you choose to talk about and however you choose to structure your podcast. Think of it like a mini radio show, available 24/7, and offering bite-sized segments for listeners to consume. Could you start a podcast to engage your audience? Could you find opportunities to be interviewed on other podcasters' shows with your message and expertise? It's something to consider, as people look online more and more to find what they're looking for.

Getting Interviews

Like I mentioned, being interviewed on podcasts can help greatly to promote yourself as an author (and your message/vision). Being interviewed anywhere is an opportunity for people you wouldn't normally reach yourself to hear about you and your book.

In reality, listeners want to hear your message, wisdom, experiences, solutions, kindness, ideas, strategies, creativity, or inspiration. They don't really want to hear about your book initially. Always keep that in mind as you look for interview opportunities. Show hosts, bloggers, podcasters, Facebook group admins, etc., are only looking for people to highlight who can add value to their show, blog, group, community, organization, or listener audience. Your book isn't their priority; their audience's needs is their priority. Once people hear your message and get to know you, then they may become interested in getting your book.

Where can you find interviews as an author?

Podcasts   YouTube channels
Radio shows   Magazines
Facebook groups   e-newsletters
Blogs   Newspapers
TV   Broadcasts for organizations

There are so many opportunities, but realize not every show or blog out there is a good fit for interviewing you. As I mentioned, each show has a theme and an audience that is the priority. What you have to offer and talk on must be a good match for that audience.

When you secure interviews, most likely the host will want these things from you:

Headshot author photo   A PDF version of your book
Book cover image (front)   Your short bio
Link to buy your book   Interview questions

Be prepared with these items and you'll exude professionalism. And speaking of professionalism, have a good-quality author photo of yourself. That picture your neighbor took of you at last year's potluck probably won't cut it!

Getting some interview practice before real interviews is important. Show hosts want to feel confident that their guests will make a good impression and not have frustrating quirks. I used to host an Internet radio show and would interview lots of interesting people several times a month. One author I interviewed, a very nice woman, said "ya know" about 42 times during the interview. Let's just say...that's not ideal.

Because I was not comfortable with public speaking or interviews as a new author, I took a public speaking class. I also practiced talking and answering pretend questions while in the car, alone in my room or at my desk. It helped me a lot. Have a friend or two give you some interview practice. Record yourself answering mock questions and listen closely for unnecessary filler words or phrases or if you stumbled in answering quickly at any point. Have certain types of answers ready on the tip of your tongue. Interviews are a very helpful tool for an author's marketing plan. We do some author interview practice at IPWA from time to time, and it's helpful.

Book Reviewers

Some websites and blogs exist to review books. Some bloggers and podcasters frequently review books related to their show/blog's topic and audience. Many of these opportunities come at a price; you pay to have your book reviewed and highlighted. Depending on the site/show and their audience, it could be worth it. If you have a compelling pitch to shows and bloggers, you may be able to get a free review if, and usually only if, it fits their audience and theme well. This is another chance to think about any show hosts, email list owners, influencers or bloggers you know personally. Would they be willing to do a book review for you?

Also important when it comes to reviewers is getting your readers to leave reviews on bookselling websites (like Amazon). Getting reader reviews is very valuable, and can help boost your book's placement in search results. On your website, you could even have a page dedicated to reader feedback and testimonials.

Launch Strategy

As your book publishing process progresses and is nearly complete, this is when it's time to coordinate your book launch efforts. When your book is done, ready for sale and you want to tell the world about it, this is what's referred to as its launch. Most authors choose a specific launch date; a date on which to start promoting the book and telling others that it's out and available for sale.

What I don't recommend is waiting until your book is already published and available for sale to then figure out how you're going to promote it. Instead, plan ahead. As with nearly every aspect of an author's book journey, planning your book launch has many, many different potential strategies. Again, there's no possible way to touch on them all here in this book. However, below are a few ideas to get you started; things to think about beforehand.

What day will your book officially be launched?
Where will you direct people to purchase it?
Will you do a presale?
Who can help you get the word out?
How can you start to talk about it now?
What can I build or put in place now that will help me have a ready audience?

Let's talk about these a bit.

In order for you to plan the launch, the number one question is *when*. If it's late February and you're still writing, with approximately four more weeks of writing and reviewing to go, but you have editing help and a graphic designer for your cover already lined up, you may be able to estimate a launch date of sometime in late May. It gives you something to shoot for and helps with planning. It also holds your feet (or fingers in this case) to the fire to get it done. Once you announce that your book will be out in May, it adds motivation and accountability. We need that!

Authors have two main options for their launch (and every other time) for where they direct potential buyers to buy their books: either at an online book-selling site or from the author directly. You can certainly do both—have your books available at online book sites and sell them yourself—but many times, authors want to direct people to one spot during their launch timeframe.

During your launch, when you direct readers to buy your book from Amazon (Kindle and/or print), your book has the opportunity to hit some of their bestseller lists in the genres you select. Also, Amazon or the other sites will process payments and ship books out with every order, meaning you don't have to.

When you direct people to purchase directly from you, you make a bit more profit, although it requires more work (processing payments, shipping books out, etc.). Despite the extra work, you will get to collect your buyers' email and other information. This is a plus. When your book sells online at Amazon, Apple books, Barnes & Noble or other book-selling sites, unfortunately you'll never know who bought it. You can also tout the copies you sell yourself as signed copies and send a personal note or more information along with the book.

Note: you won't be able to sell Kindle, Nook or Apple Books-version eBooks directly. Your option for personally selling an e-version of your book is limited to a PDF file sent via email or downloadable off your site.

Have you thought of pre-selling your printed book before it comes out? Have you thought of doing a preorder for your book on Amazon? Both of these options work a bit differently, but both or either may be a great option for you. If you have an audience ready to read your book, offering it for sale even before it's out is an idea you should consider.

One method, pre-selling printed copies people will buy from you, allows you to get some revenue and helps to determine how many books to have printed in your initial book order. If you get 50 presales, people are paying retail prices, but you're buying printed copies at print wholesale pricing. If you make a profit of $10 per copy when you sell your book yourself, that would be $500. If it costs you $4 per copy, you'll buy those 50 presale copies for just $200. With the $300 profit, you could order another 50 copies to sell later and still have $100 left.

Setting up a preorder on Amazon (for your Kindle version) will be another option, and I recommend you research it on Amazon's KDP help area. They change their requirements and processes on occasion, so going directly there will give you the most current information on how it works. Check out their requirements early. As of right now, setting up a preorder requires some lead time. You aren't able to set it up and have it start immediately, and it must fall within a certain timeframe before your book is released. A big question you should ask yourself is *who can help me get the word out about my book when it's out?* Many people who know you will be willing to help in some way. At the very least, your friends and family members will probably agree to let others know about your new book either via email or their social media accounts. Make it easy for them. Create a post they can share, create a graphic with your book cover they can post, make a flyer they can forward and give them the link to where your book can be purchased.

You can consider the people willing to help spread the word about your book's release your "launch team." Whether you have extremely organized ideas or a more lax approach to how these willing people can help, keep your launch team up-to-date with information, dates and links they need to have. There are ways to get proof or galley copies (or even a PDF version) out to pre-launch readers, known as advanced reader copies (ARCs). These readers can be helpful to have with their reviews and help with promotion. You could even just share a chapter or two with them as a preview to get them excited.

Who else could help you during your launch? Do you have friends, clients, co-workers, business partners, schools, ministries, or associations who could let their networks know? Is there someone you know who could interview you? Are there communities and groups on Facebook that would post about your book? Could you and someone with a complimentary service, book or product do a cross promotion? Will you want to pay for promotion help?

Your launch strategy can include paying for a book promotion service like BookBub, eBook Stage and Bargain Booksy. Do some research on services like these. These services have huge email lists and communities of Kindle readers. Authors launching new books can advertise their low-priced or free Kindle version with these services for a few days and see a spike in sales. Because these services want free or low-cost eBooks, using these marketing services can't be for the purpose of making lots of money on sales. Instead, the intent would need to be attracting new readers, getting your message out to many quickly, getting best-seller status in your genre's category or other notoriety.

Let me touch on being a bestseller for a moment. You've probably heard many people calling themselves a "best-selling author" or their book a "best-selling book." Despite what other people who market their services and groups to authors may tell you, being considered a bestseller is really not that difficult to accomplish these days. With a little strategy and coordination to rally your friends, family, clients, and other people in your network for your launch week, you should be able to achieve this status on Amazon.

What constitutes being a bestseller? Your book, print or e-version, must reach the best-seller list (top 100 titles) for one or more of the categories it's listed in. Of course, this is based on sales numbers, although Amazon also has a free Kindle book best-seller list as well. Building your platform and audience now can help greatly with rallying people to buy your book during your launch week.

All along your book planning, writing and publishing steps, you can be already thinking about building your platform (and doing it). You've probably heard this *platform* concept before. In a nutshell, a platform is somewhere where you are communicating and someone is paying attention, someone is listening. Platforms come in all shapes and sizes today, things like blogs, speaking opportunities with real stages (conferences, events, meetings, trainings, etc.), interviews, podcasts, blogs, YouTube channels, radio shows, Facebook groups and communities, social media accounts with specific themes, mentoring groups, rallies, community events, online events like summits, workshops, challenges, masterclasses, or other trainings, etc. If you have a message, written, spoken, in-person or online, someone somewhere wants to hear it. Who are they, and where are they?

Right now, you can be building a platform where you'll have a ready-made audience who's interested in your book's message. Use your platform to create and gather this community of people. If you have something to write to this audience, if you have a heart for this group of people, if you want to inspire, entertain, mentor or inform them through your book, you can certainly start talking about it now.

With that thought, let's wrap up this chapter on book/author marketing ideas. Although this chapter is in no way a comprehensive dive into all the potential options for marketing your book, it's a great place to begin.

Chapter Eight:

Summary and Next Steps

If you've read this far, congratulations! To me, your reading commitment indicates you are serious about being an author and you want to get the advice and knowledge you need to be successful. There is still much to know.

"Unless commitment is made, there are only promises and hopes; but no plans." —Peter F. Drucker

For some people, being an author is a calling. For some, writing and storytelling is where their creativity lies. For others, they feel compelled to tell their story and impact people. Still for others, being an author is a hobby. Whether you write as a hobby, have a calling or hope to make writing your full-time work, all of those take dedication, know-how and help.

For those who like the idea of being able to self-publish as many books as they have in their hearts and minds, it's very possible. You can do it with a little support and know-how. Like learning to ride a bike when you were six or to drive when you were 15, this author thing can be mastered and won't be perplexing anymore!

If you'd like some structure, accountability, training and community, I'd like to invite you to join us at the International Prophetic Writers Association. We have monthly or yearly membership options available. Our goal is to offer authors a supportive community of like-missioned people where they can learn, collaborate, improve their skills, discover new strategies and ideas, find helpful resources, and so much more.

Our online program walks authors through the whole process of developing, writing, publishing and marketing books, with an emphasis on learning the self-publishing process. No matter how many books you have to write in the future, our program will help prepare you, giving you the knowledge you need in order to manage your self-publishing process with less expense.

Interested in online learning? Want to be part of a supportive author community and get questions answered? Want access to live, weekly online training classes? There are many ways to connect with us at IPWA, including enrolling. If you're interested in learning more, IPWA's enrollment details can be found on an upcoming page.

But first, think about this. As authors, we have a great opportunity. Our voice and message in written form can be far-reaching, going even beyond our lifetimes. We have a weighty responsibility. Our words will influence others, even those we may never meet. We have a unique creative outlet and expression. Authorship affords us a special way to release the gifts, messages, creativity and wisdom God has placed inside each of us. Being an author is an amazing thing.

After the many things I've done in my lifetime, I believe:

#AuthorLife is the best life.

What will author life look like for you? I hope it is filled with joy and a confident satisfaction, knowing you've written many books your readers love and have made a meaningful difference in the lives of others.

Here's to you and your author journey! May bountiful words flow out of you to impact and inspire your readers. Thank you for reading this book. It was a work of passion and joy. Many blessings to you.

Krista Dunk
Author, publisher, founder of the International Prophetic Writers Association
www.KristaDunk.com
www.internationalpwa.com

About IPWA

The International Prophetic Writers Association is an online author school and community powered by 100X Publishing and is connected to the 100X community of Kingdom entrepreneurs founded by Pedro and Suzette Adao and Emerging Prophets founded by Keith Ferrante. Our goal is to serve authors, aspiring authors, and prophetic writers, offering them supportive community, comprehensive training, how-to steps, new ideas and strategies, resources and links, and much more so authors can master self-publishing in order to write, publish and sell as many books as they have in their hearts to write. We have several enrollment options, including a monthly enrollment option for authors looking for a month-to-month sign-up commitment.

Opportunities to connect with IPWA:

Free #AuthorLife News weekly newsletter
Free worksheets and handouts for authors:
www.internationalpwa.com/freeworksheets
Join an upcoming 3-Day Write Your Book Challenge session:
www.kristadunk.com/3-daychallenge

Monthly Self-Starter enrollment: $97
Yearly Self-Starter enrollment: $997
Premium Yearly Coaching Plus+ enrollment: $1997

Monthly Self-Starter enrollment:
Full access to our online member learning portal (videos, handouts, templates, resources and links, and more), weekly training classes, private members-only Facebook community, free admission to Krista's author challenges/classes (for current members), and members-only discounts from publishing service providers.

Yearly Self-Starter enrollment:
One year of full access to our online learning portal (videos, handouts, templates, resources and links, and more), weekly training classes, private members-only Facebook community, free admission to any of Krista's author challenges/classes (for current members), and members-only discounts from publishing service providers.

Interested in also having some personal coaching? Want someone to review your completed manuscript? Want help with some publishing services? All of these are available to monthly and yearly regular members at additional cost. Check out our premium, yearly Coaching Plus+ enrollment option which includes these automatically.

Premium Coaching Plus+ yearly enrollment:
One-year full access to everything included in our regular self-starter yearly enrollment, plus six, 30-minute personal coaching sessions, 90 minutes of manuscript review, an author interview, and quarterly #AuthorLife merchandise OR $1,000 in publishing services to help you finalize your book files for publishing.

You are invited to join us!

"Earlier this year, I knew I had a book in me, but I was stuck. I didn't know how to start, what kind of book or what was involved. Krista was offering a 10-day challenge on getting a book started. Although I met her in person at an event the year before, I didn't know much about how she could help, but I was hoping to find out. I was blown away. The first day of the challenge, the light bulb went on. Within 24 hours, an outline was done. The guidance and support Krista has given me enabled me to focus on the story and complete it within a few weeks. Then came editing, publishing, artwork and more. Whew, who knew all that was needed to get a book published! Krista was so key in helping me navigate all the steps, and her encouragement kept me going. I highly recommend 100X Publishing, the Academy and Krista to any budding or experienced authors."
—Donald Wickham, *Elle and the Secret of the Magic Pillars*

"I knew I was supposed to write my memoir but had no clue where to begin. With all the effort going into writing a book, I wanted to do it with excellence. I saw an ad for a "21-Day Finish Your Book Challenge" on Facebook led by Krista Dunk, and knew immediately I needed to join. In her challenge she covered every aspect of writing, publishing options, layout, style, character development, voice, transition, covers, etc. Most importantly, Krista is a phenomenal teacher and listener. She carries great wisdom and grace and is a wealth of knowledge. If you are wanting to write your first book or have written one in the past and felt frustrated in the process, I highly recommend you get under Krista's mentorship in the Academy. The world needs to hear what you have to say and she will help you do it with excellence."
—*Pastor Patti Helzer, Choosing to Live Free*

Recommended Resources

Designrr – software for creating amazing eBooks.
https://bit.ly/2Ylfe7O

100X Acceleration – online community and training for faith-based entrepreneurs, marketing training, personal and spiritual development. https://bit.ly/31jeiSX

Amazon's author account set up and training: kdp.amazon.com.

IngramSpark author account set up and training: www.ingramspark.com

Scrivener – an organizational system for authors. https://bit.ly/2Z1ROor

Kartra – online platform for creating websites, funnels, email lists and much more. https://bit.ly/31noNo5

Canva – great tool to create flyers, logos, graphics, find stock photos, etc. https://bit.ly/31qqe5j

BookBaby – publishing services, printing and distribution option offering authors extra help. https://bit.ly/3kksh2s

ACX – learn how to create and upload audiobooks for sale online. www.acx.com

Notes and Ideas

Use this section to start planning and capturing your ideas for your book project(s)!

Book Idea: _____

What's it about?
Message/Theme: _____

Who needs to read it?
Audience: _____
Reader age range: _____
Boys, girls, men, women: _____

Non-fiction: your readers' pain points are:
_____
What they think they want/what you know they need:
_____

Fiction: genre _____
Their hobbies and interests: _____
Other similar books they like: _____
_____

Notes:

Book Idea: _____

What's it about?
Message/Theme: _____

Who needs to read it?
Audience: _____
Reader age range: _____
Boys, girls, men, women: _____

Non-fiction: your readers' pain points are:
_____
What they think they want/what you know they need:
_____

Fiction: genre _____
Their hobbies and interests: _____
Other similar books they like: _____
_____

Notes:

About the Author

Krista Dunk is an author, speaker, the project director for two book publishing companies, and founder of the International Prophetic Writers Association. A teacher at heart, Krista has written 12 books so far. Her first book, *Step Out and Take Your Place*, was published in early 2011. Along with her first book, its companion resources and *Author Acceleration*, she has also published a devotional, the *Ninja Kitty* children's book series, books in The Abundance Plan book series, an anthology book called *Broken Chapters,* and *The Prophetic Writer's Book Ideas Journal.*

As a child and young adult who struggled with timidity, Krista now finds herself speaking and training in front of audiences large and small. She is passionate about helping people get a vision for how their life could look and to step out into it. Working with authors since 2012 has been one of Krista's greatest joys.

Krista and Chris, her husband of 31 years, live in Washington State and have two amazing young-adult children.

Learn more at:
www.KristaDunk.com
www.internationalpwa.com
www.FindingTruthPropheticNetwork.com

Speaking

Looking for a speaker or trainer for your conference, workshop, summit, online class, challenge, or other event? Looking to host a special workshop or need a custom training for your group or team? Connect with Krista Dunk today!

Krista is a fun, welcoming, experienced and organized speaker/trainer who loves to help people get breakthrough in the area of writing, publishing, expressing their messages and creativity.

Book-Related Training Topic Examples:
Creating Your Book's Purpose Statement
Book-Based Business Strategies
The 12 Steps of Self-Publishing
Working With Amazon
Ten Ways to Self-Edit and Review Your Manuscript
Why Write a Book?
The Freedom to Tell Your Stories
Discussing her own author journey
Prophetic Writing from Victory

To contact Krista regarding speaking engagements and interviews, send a note now to info@kristadunk.com.

Thank you, readers! Reader reviews are valuable, and I would greatly appreciate your book review on Amazon. To review this book, simply scan this QR code with your smart phone, and it will take you to the book's page on Amazon:

Use the following code to review this book on Goodreads:

Exclusive Publishing for Kingdom Entrepreneurs

www.100Xacademy.com